# A B C's
## of
# Teaching

## A guide for teachers

Page Pond
Press

## By
## Susan Larned Womble

Published by Page Pond Press
www.pagepondpress.com

I have tried to share real life school situations and conversations from my memories. In order to maintain anonymity and to share a point about teacher attributes, I may have changed some identifying characteristics and details.

Disclaimer: The strategies and advice herein may not be suitable for your situation. You should consult a professional when appropriate.

Cover design from clip art **www.pixabay.com** from this free source that provides license free artwork for commercial use.

Inside clip art: Artwork from Pixabay.com and other free sources that provide license free artwork for commercial use.

ISBN: **0990760049**

ISBN-13: **978-0990760047**
First Edition

Printed in the United States of America
ISBN: **0990760049**

ISBN-13: **978-0990760047**

# DEDICATION

For Thomas and Amanda

# CONTENTS

# FIRST NOTES

My personal stories in this book are inspired from first hand experiences that I have changed, added to, mixed together or deleted information for sharing purposes.

I do not profess to be the "guru" of teachers. The opinions expressed in the ABC book are just that—my opinions, gathered from my experiences as a teacher. Please read with that in mind. I hope you find some of the information useful. The clip art cartoons are an attempt to infuse humor into the reading. First and foremost, I want to encourage people to be teachers. I love teaching and want to see more people choosing teaching as a career. It is with that positive spirit that I hope you enjoy and find information you can use from this ABC book for teachers.

# ACKNOWLEDGMENTS

I acknowledge my support group, my family: Gregg, Thomas, Amanda, Harper, Grayson, Mike, Tommy and Judi for always being there. A special shout out to two of my favorite teachers; my children, Thomas and Amanda.

Thanks especially to all of the teachers, administrators, Aides, staff, and support school personnel for making teaching fun and rewarding. Thanks to my writer's group Rhett DeVane, Peggy Kassees, Evelyna Rogers, Liz Jameson, Mary Lois Sanders, Pat O'Connell, Debbie Hooper, and Gina Edwards for all of their suggestions and help. To Adrian Fogelin, Perky Granger and all of the St George writing retreat buddies for keeping me inspired and on track. And a special thanks to my Beta Readers and idea people: Tina Pipp, Katie Clark, and Peggy Kelly.

# The ABC's of Teaching

Wouldn't it be great if you could take a pill that would make you a great teacher? It'd be even better if the pill were chocolate flavored.

Ever wonder what magic formula makes a successful teacher. Guess what? There is no magic formula or magic pill. But, I hope this book will help you become a successful teacher. This book, organized in ABC form, concentrates on characteristics I have observed over my career as a teacher. Some positive and some negative. I hope you see yourself more in the positive traits, rather than the negative. Don't beat yourself up though because let's be honest we have all had days that we projected one or more of these undesirable qualities. This is a hard look at different characteristics of teachers from a firsthand perspective.

Each topic is divided alphabetically. An appendix is added at the end of the book for topic organization. Teacher traits follow a specific guideline. Each attribute is explained, first by an opinion based on personal experience along with a teacher story where applicable, and then by a visual.

## A

Attention to Detail: For teachers, just like many other professions, attention to detail is important. Teachers use a lot of modeling to show students what they want them to emulate. If teachers are sloppy and don't make sure that the details are crisp and correct, then the student will copy inaccurate work. Enlist experts to explain for a more in-depth understanding of the lesson concept. Another reason teachers need to have attention to details is because they are responsible for deciphering the student's potential. What does that mean? When a teacher is assigned a student, he or she can process the student's strengths and weaknesses from the previous year's assessments. The teacher has to be able to develop a plan that will enable said student grasp the concept being taught. Teachers are expected to draw conclusions about the best approach for individual students. This cannot be accomplished without attention to detail.

Always on time: As simple as it sounds, it is so important to be on time. There are only a few jobs where so many others depend on your timeliness. I can only remember over sleeping one time. I woke up at home five minutes after the tardy bell rang, I called the school to tell them. They assured me they would send coverage and to come through the office when I arrived. When I got to school and signed in, I found out they had called down on the speaker in my classroom to let my students know that someone was coming to cover class. But before they could give the students the message, one of the students yelled, "Mrs. Womble is not here. She went to the bathroom. She'll be back in a minute." I loved that my students had so sweetly tried to cover for me. Their hearts were in the right place. Funnier still is the comradery I felt with the students. Perceptions of a tug of war with my students did not always ring true. We were all on the same side. Promptness is an important life skill to teach your students. If being on time is a problem for you, then teaching may not be your thing.

Class will start in 10 minutes, I have to get to my classroom to stand at the door.

Isn't the time schedule just a suggestion? I'll be there some time after the last bell sounds.

<u>Asks Questions:</u> Don't be afraid to ask questions. Many things will be explained during those first days, but not everything is addressed. Ask questions. If you are a new teacher or new to a school or moved to a new classroom, ask questions like: What's my budget? Where do I get copies? Can I throw away things in my room that I don't plan on using or if not where should they be stored or sent? I remember mentoring a new teacher and when we went to her class, the file cabinets were full of old files, some of them from the mimeograph days. There were old books on the shelves. It was a mess. I spent most of my first meeting with her cleaning out her room after we found out what we could do with the stuff. Side note for teachers leaving or retiring, clean out your room. Lots of teachers are afraid to throw out stuff.

I'm up under here, I promise. I'm looking for my lesson plans. They are in here somewhere. Do you think I could get rid of this phone? I think it's been here since the 1950's.

Aware of all school staff: There are other people on staff besides classroom teachers and administrators. There are secretaries, bookkeepers, janitors, Aides, project people, district facilitators, assistants to a variety of people, curriculum professionals, technology experts, media specialists, guidance counselors and that's just scratching the surface. It is important to be patient at a school new to you. If you wait, who actually knows everything about the school will become apparent to you. If you want to know something or who you should ask, always check with the front office first. They will most likely be able to steer you in the right direction. They are the heart of the school. The cleanup crew is very important also as they are the ones who have keys to everything and will be there if you accidently lock yourself out. Or if you have an unexpected throw up or if someone spills the science experiment. Or if the air-conditioner or heater breaks in your classroom. They may not be able to fix it, but they know who to call.

Who knows everything about everything? The principal? You would think so but NOT SO FAST! The Teachers? That would be nice, but NO! It's the bookkeeper. She knows about everything.

Always late: I know I've already addressed time, but it is SO important. Some teachers have a tendency to be late. There are many jobs in which a person can be late; teaching is not one of those professions. I remember a teacher who rolled in late most days. Her first period started in coming late too. She also skipped her morning duty that she shared with another teacher. The administration found out about the lateness when there was a morning fight in the lunchroom. Following up, the administrator searched for comments from the two teachers on duty. Not finding the missing teacher, he went to her first period class. He confronted her as she came in late with her purchased coffee in hand. She was immediately reprimanded and her pay docked. She was not late for the rest of the year, but was not rehired. It doesn't matter how great a teacher you are if you don't show up. Let this be a cautionary tale for those of you who are habitually late. Your students must be on time, why shouldn't you?

Attention Seeker:   In my years of teaching, I've noticed that there are some people who dominate meetings whether it's a small intimate three people meeting, full blown faculty meeting, or a department meeting. It really doesn't matter, they feel what they say is much more important than what anyone else has to say. I have to admit that this could be part of what makes them want to be a teacher. If you think about it, in teaching you have a captive audience of 30 or so students that HAVE to listen to the teacher. The part that craves that attention is fed on a daily basis.  Back to the meetings, there is not much of a way to stop this attention seeker in your role as a teacher. Your administration or department head has to curb the teacher. What can you do to make your voice heard? You can write down ideas to share with those in charge. This is a way to have your voice heard. This also allows opportunity for those in charge to edit the suggestion.  It is hoped that if accepted, the recipient will give credit where credit is due—a hazard of giving suggestions. I cannot tell you the amount of times that I have heard new or beginning teachers refuse to give a suggestion because they do not think they have had enough experience as a teacher to have a useful point of view. Without the new voices, how will the school ever grow?

<u>Afraid to keep up with changing times:</u>  Can you think of how many times you have wished that all of the administrators or those people at the Department of Education would come back into the classroom for just a day to see what is like before they make rules and changes that affect you on a daily basis? Teachers have the freshest voices and ideas and should be given a safe platform in which to express said ideas. We change textbooks often because we want to keep up with the times. We have in-services to continue improving. Shouldn't we want to improve and keep up with the changing world? Be the expert in your classroom. We are constantly being thrown new strategies, materials, standards, or programs to try. There is a barrage of NEW stuff every year. A big challenge is not to take on too many changes at once. Force yourself to be selective and focus on what strategy to implement that is best for "your kids." The hope is that you will have a principal who respects your expertise and does not micromanage. Introducing new and fresh ideas improves and allows classroom lessons to grow. We ask that students constantly improve. We ask them to try even if they fail as a way to grow. Can we ask any less of ourselves as teachers? Be the EXPERT.

All teachers should: teach, invent curriculum, make detailed behavior plans, implement those plans, keep up on the latest research, all while making sure each student learns at his or her pace and enters every bit of information on this very specific computerized program.

Come be the teacher for a day, then tell me how to do all of that.

<u>Assembly Dodger:</u> Part of any school is assemblies, whether it be sports assemblies, listening to guest speakers, or assemblies to cheer on the team. It is a time for the entire school to get together. Not only is it important to listen to the message conveyed, it is also a bonding time. For a student to feel like they are part of something, they must BE part of something. Accompany your students to assemblies to be part of something bigger than just your class. You are part of a faculty, not just part of your class. Too many times teachers feel as if they are an island. Granted you are responsible for your specific class, but aren't you also responsible for making the school itself successful? There are so many useful traits for the students to learn in assemblies; they learn to behave in a group setting. They learn to ignore bad behaviors. They learn to listen. These attributes will serve them well in later years, whether it be in the 400 person lecture in college or a one-on-one interview for a future job. If they don't learn to sit and listen early, then they won't develop that skill. When you don't attend these assemblies, you send the message that assemblies aren't important and are not to be taken seriously. That's not true. Don't steal this learning opportunity from them because you do not deem it important or because you have not managed your time wisely. This is part of the school and should not be an option. When I first started teaching, I remember many teachers asking me to watch their students during assemblies for the entire time. Don't do this. It's unprofessional.

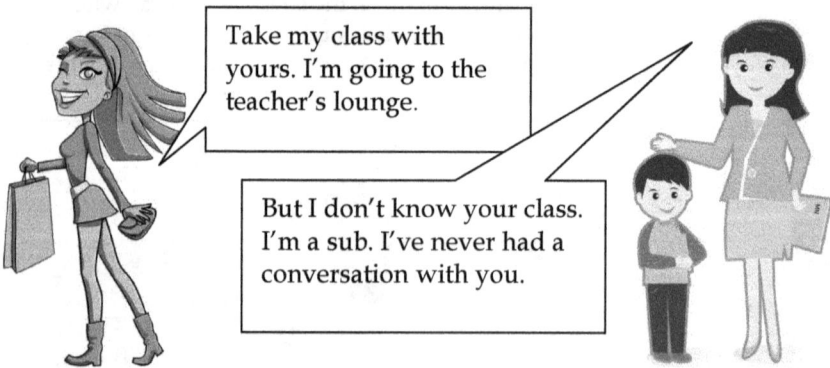

Take my class with yours. I'm going to the teacher's lounge.

But I don't know your class. I'm a sub. I've never had a conversation with you.

Adopter of students: Teachers are caregivers by nature, but it is important to stay in your lane. You are not the student's parent and you must try to work with the parents of your students. It is best if all are on the same page. If you want the student to succeed, you need to enlist support from the parents, if possible. The best thing you can do as a teacher is to find something positive to say about the student when talking to his or her parents on the phone or during meetings. Before lambasting the student for inappropriate behavior, concentrate on the positive attributes. Look hard, there is always something. For example, I had a student who was always giggling and being silly in class, but was not serious about his work and his grades suffered. Instead of trying to parent the student, I relied on the support of his parent. I called the parent and the first thing I told her was her child was very pleasant and that he could probably have a successful career as a standup comic in the future, but in the classroom he needed to be serious about his work. The parent worked with me. We developed a sign off sheet that he took home daily for reporting appropriate or inappropriate behavior. I gave him 10 minutes as a reward where he could do jokes, rap, or something else to entertain the other students. He had to follow rules for his stand up that included no bullying or making fun of others. It worked out very well. Sometimes instead of adopting students as your own, think outside the box. And always remember, what works for one might not work for all.

Josie, is your mother coming to the parent teacher meeting?

No, I didn't tell Mom because Ms. Mathers, my math teacher, said she would come.

Absences—Too many: As a teacher, it is important for you to come to work. Believe me, everyone will notice if you are always absent on Mondays or Fridays. This is a job. I'm not saying to never take a personal day or mental health day. Sometimes you just need a day off, but not every Monday and Friday. Your students will suffer. The curriculum is set up to accomplish something every day. That is hard to do if you always have a sub. If you can give hand outs and not teach, then you need to take a long hard look at your lessons. Also, there is usually a set amount of sub money allocated for each school each year. I have been at a school where they ran out of sub money simply because there were too many teachers taking more days off than were allocated for them. Most schools have generous leave time. Don't abuse it. You not only hurt your students, you could hurt the school's budget. And you hurt your reputation sometimes beyond repair. I knew a teacher who had a health issue and it was a long drawn out negotiation with the district to find money to supply her classroom with a temporary substitute because of abuse of leave time. Stress for all concerned. Think about the domino effect your actions might have on others.

I know I've taken off every Monday and Friday, but I need to recuperate. Plus there's something wrong with my pay, I haven't had a full month's pay since I've been at this school.

And you don't know why? Hmm…

Authority Issues: Teachers are in charge in their classrooms. Department heads have authority over their departments. Assistant Principals have authority over certain parts of the school such as curriculum, discipline, or student support. Assistant Principals might also have authority over some teachers. The Principal has authority over the staff and teachers at their prospective schools. It is important to understand the hierarchy of authority. The reason there is a chart of who is in charge is to help the school run smoothly. If something goes wrong at the school, then there must be a person who is responsible for it all. I have been around teachers who buck the system at every turn. They are always challenging even the most mundane request. This can be a problem at a school. Schools are dependent on comradery and everybody being on the same page to run smoothly. You don't want to be deemed a troublemaker. If you have a problem with a request, take it through the proper channels. You can also ask why or talk to a union rep, but what you can't do is refuse unless the request is somehow detrimental or inappropriate in some sort of way to you as a person. If you want to make the final decisions at the school, you might want to begin an employment tract as an administrator.

# B

<u>Bender of Rules</u>: Follow your administrator's rules, especially new teachers. You might have great ideas about how to change things, but remember the buck stops with your administrators. It is their school. If things go bad, it falls on them to answer for it. Their job is to lead their teachers and make sure they follow the rules. Most of the time, rules have been developed by your state's Department of Education, by your district, or department administration. I have attended parent meetings where the teachers comes in, no grade book, no student tests, just expecting to say how they think the student is doing in class. This is not professional. You must have data to back up your claims. The only way to generate grades is to have items to grade. The grade cannot be just a guess. You cannot conduct your class on how you feel the student has grasped the information. Think about how you would have felt in your college classes if your professor just wanted to give grades by their feelings of how you did. Be careful. Some parents are very litigious. They look for ways to sue the district. You must be careful not to give grounds for a lawsuit. For example, sending a student home early every day for poor behavior is not an answer. Look to develop a behavior plan or something else. Not following the rules is a big no-no so be careful.

I couldn't find your semester grades on our grade smart program.

Oh, I haven't given any tests. I just guesstimate how I think the students did and give grades at the end of the 9 weeks. My favorites always get an 'A.'

Bulletin Board Crazy: Really artsy teachers love bulletin boards. Your bulletin boards are a nice addition to your class. Interactive bulletin boards can be used to supplement a lesson or showcase student work. You can highlight school themes, current vocabulary, and anchor charts. Problems arise when teachers would rather make bulletin boards than teach class. Also, bulletin boards take materials, construction paper, printer ink, etc. This can become a problem if your class is using all of the supplies. Most schools have a budget for materials. This budget has to cover copy paper, pens, pencils, notebook paper, construction paper, printer ink, etc. It is selfish of you to use more than your share. If you are spending your own money on supplies, it can be quite costly. Creative teachers are encouraged to stay in the profession. If it costs you too much, no matter how much you love teaching, it will seem like you are spinning your wheels in terms of money. It also takes time to change bulletin boards. Time you may not have. We don't want to lose teachers because they are spending all of their time on lessons, bulletin boards, etc. and not enough time for themselves or their families. Manage your time effectively. One tip I can give you is to make a bulletin board a semester or every 9 weeks for the first year. Save those bulletin boards. Be careful storing them. Put them in big zip lock bags. Then the next year add two more and within 5 years you will have enough to change all the time. Just a thought.

I'm so excited for my lesson today. My students and I are making a new bulletin board.

Didn't you just put up a new bulletin board two days ago?

Being Cognizant of Students from Different Backgrounds:
Teachers need to be aware that their student will be coming
from all kinds of backgrounds. There will be military students,
delinquents, preppy, students of helicopter parents, different
culture, races, religions, sheltered, latch-key, and free
thinking, to name a few. The different types of backgrounds of
your students will run the gamut of the types of people in the
world. You must try to keep an open mind and be aware if
something is off. Ask questions of the student. See if you can
discover what the issues are. Sometimes problems have to do
with the class, but a lot of times they don't. I had two students
fight the minute they got to school. The argument had started
in their neighborhood and spilled over into the school
environment. There were consequences, but my point is that
you must be aware that we only have the students for 6 to 7
hours a day. The rest of the time they are experiencing their
own lives. Be respectful of others and the way they live and
think. And teach your students to be respectful of others
different from them.

Bringing in Snack Foods: It's important to remember your students are on the same schedule as you. Eating in front of your students is rude if they don't have food. I have seen teachers who eat constantly. They stand up, give a five-minute lesson, hand out a paper or assign bookwork, and then sit at their desk and eat. I ask you to think about what you would do if after you gave your lesson, your students pulled out a sandwich or a drink and ate at their desk. Don't abuse being an adult. Think of it as a package of gum. If you are sitting and talking to three friends and you pull out gum. You are more than likely to ask each of those three if they want some gum. It's good etiquette. Be aware of your students' feelings. It is perfectly acceptable to eat when you have lunch or breakfast duty. That being said, feel free to pig out during planning or duty free time in your classroom before or after school. But remember that the smell will linger on so maybe be nice and throw your trash out in a receptacle outside of your room. I always liked to eat in the teacher's lounge if I didn't have lunch duty as it was a nice time for comradery with other teachers.

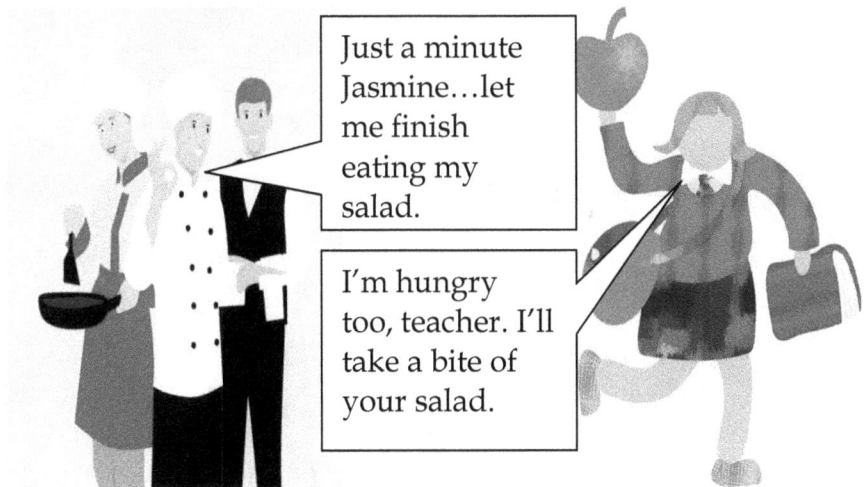

Just a minute Jasmine…let me finish eating my salad.

I'm hungry too, teacher. I'll take a bite of your salad.

Bathroom Time Management Or Being Able to go the Bathroom Quickly: An important time management issue for teachers is taking care of bathroom needs. Unless you have an aide or another teacher available to stand in your classroom, you need to train yourself to use the bathroom during break, planning period, change of class, lunch, etc. Even though most schools have bathrooms that are set aside for adult use, I have seen very few schools that divide the bathrooms by sexes. That means that if you do some smelly business, the science teacher might come in after you. Training your body can be difficult to do. I hope this doesn't sound too crass, but let me offer a suggestion for the times you might want more privacy. Make sure that you think about what you eat and coach yourself to have a time to go at the same time every day and hopefully that particular time is in the privacy of your home. Or if unable to do this, at least scout the school out for the most private bathroom available.

Sorry I couldn't talk to you when you called this morning. It was my morning bathroom time.

Too much information

Benchmark, Assessments, Standards Accountability: With all of the accountability in the school system, benchmarks, placement growth, growth charts, it's hard not to get lost in it all. I have seen some teachers that look great on paper, but are horrible in the classroom. Their lessons are perfect and they have their benchmarks or standards listed. They check all of the boxes the district wants. You must learn to manage your time to be able to hit all of these marks and still be able to teach. The formulas of what you must do are there to help you, not to hinder you. The hope is that it will help you focus your lessons towards those standards that need to be taught and learned. It is not just for show. It is supposed to be a guide. Make sure that you don't spend all of your energy on paperwork. Your teaching is the most important aspect. You should not have to invent any of these standards, guided lessons, etc. from scratch. There are a myriad of resources available to make your life easier in terms of paperwork. Make sure the bulk of your energy is spent adapting and implementing your lessons, not inventing them.

Isn't my benchmark perfect?

I see the benchmark, but I still don't know what I'm learning. What's the lesson about?

# C

Creativity: To me the best teachers are the most creative ones. Don't despair if you are not creative, fortunately most teachers are sharers. If they have a good creative lesson that meets the objectives of the classroom, they will share. I think some of my best in-service meetings were when the teachers took over the meeting and shared a particularly great lesson. The discussions would range from changing levels to changing for differentiated instruction to changing for different subjects. The discussions led to adaptions of the lessons. The ownership then reverted not just to the inventor of the lesson, but also to the group as a whole. What a great way to design a lesson. I usually came out of those meetings with a huge inventory of ideas for lessons. It was inspiration for my own creativity. Make sure to include your students or interns. I have had many an intern come up with great lesson. In fact I've had students come up with great new ideas through projects they were assigned. They would get with their group, brainstorm, and come up with a fresh approach. Do research; keep up with the ever-changing scope of education. You don't know what you might find out there that will inspire and enhance your own creativity.

We are going to do our own Olympics. Math: Diving with Integers, English: Racing for Verbs, Social Studies: Swimming with the Constitution, and Science: Floor Exercise with Planets.

<u>Constantly Changing the Design of your Room:</u>  One thing that drives me crazy is the teacher who is always changing the layout of his or her classroom.  I go in one day and the students are sitting in a circle. The next day the students' desks are lined up. Then one day they are all facing to the front, the next day they are back to back. Besides being very confusing for the students, I am not sure how these changes make any kind of sense. I understand that once in a while it's important to change. For projects, you definitely want to have your students in small groups, maybe around a table. If your lesson calls for centers, then it's important to have your room set up before students enter the classroom. But everyday or two or three times a week is too much. Think about this. Students need consistency. They like to walk into your classroom and see the first assignment; the ice breaker, morning problem, or activity to get started on their work. They want to know where to place their homework; they want to know where you'll be standing and where they're supposed to sit. I'm not saying never change it up; I'm just saying don't let it take away from your teaching.

Today, our class will be divided into a diamond on the left, a circle to the right and four separate desks at each corner unlike yesterday whereas half of you were back to back and the rest faced each other. Don't you just love it?

Where should you sit? Hmm, hadn't thought of that.

Cliques at School: It is nice to have friends at school. Although having friends at school can be detrimental to your professional life, if you let it. I can remember a time at school where we had a clique. While it was enjoyable to me and did not seem to be hurting others, I did notice one thing. I was in charge of an afterschool program and a few of my friends worked for the afterschool program. Unfortunately, what happened is that a few of these friends had excuses for not covering their afterschool assignments. As I was in charge, I would have to cover those assignments. The afterschool assignment was paid on an hourly basis. When I turned in the time sheets, my absent teacher friends still expected to be paid because I had covered for them. It was a hardship for me and for our friendship. I caution you, make sure that your friendships at school are not going to interfere with your ability to do your job. The same goes for romances within the workplace. A bad idea, but I know it happens. It's all great as long as it doesn't affect your work and it is going strong. But if anything sours, those around you suffer. Once again, a cautionary tale.

I made sure we had the same planning, lunch and after school duty time for social time.

But aren't we supposed to plan and watch students during those times?

Center Crazy: Centers are great, but they can get to be a bit much. It just like anything else; too much of any one thing is too much. Be careful not to overdo centers. While constantly switching students for little doses of review can be fun, it can also be difficult for that student who needs more time to grasp a lesson objective. The differentiated instruction has to be inserted to make sure that all students are given ample opportunity to learn. It would be ineffective to only present your lessons in one way. Most of the centers entail having two or three students at a center at a time. Maybe one of those students is just riding the coattails of others. Wouldn't it be sad if that student gets lost in the cracks? Centers can be a great addition, make sure they are not the only pony in the corral.

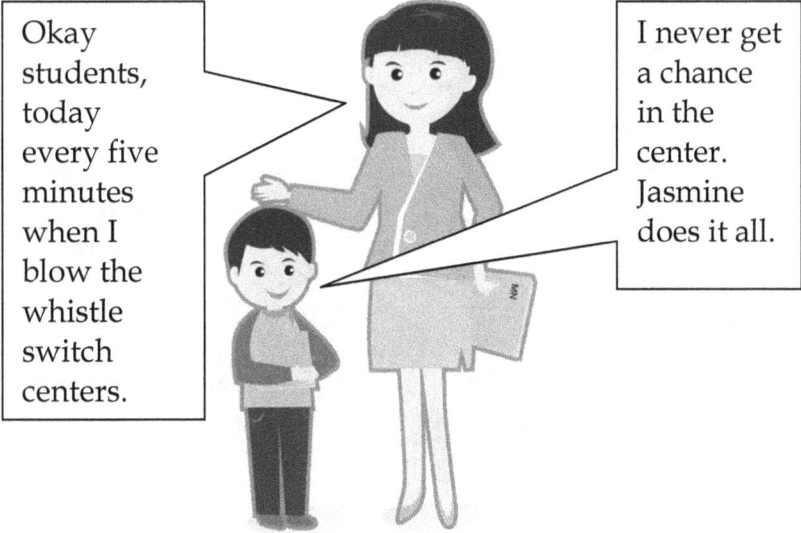

Counselor All of the Time: As caretakers, it is hard not to wear the counselor hat. I would suggest that instead you wear the facilitator hat. If a student is in need of a counselor, then send them to the proper school authority. Most schools have counselors. I had a student who got pregnant and came and asked me about getting an abortion. Students come to you because you are a teacher and are there to help them. So help them. Let the proper people handle these things. They have access to resources and student free time to help. After the student had the abortion, I'm sorry to report that she came to me again pregnant two months later. I once again took her to the proper people. She did not have a baby. I assume she was able to get some protection from pregnancy. Another time, a student came in with burn marks on her torso. I was horrified. I referred her as an emergency to our counselor. Our counselor was then able to help her. She had the time unencumbered of students to spend with this student to make sure that the student had enough time to be comfortable to share her story. Some stories can make your skin crawl. If you don't feel that horror, then you are not in the right profession.

I'm sorry class. Talk amongst yourselves. I can't teach today, Sadie needs some personal one on one attention from me. We will be in my office.

So no test on Friday since we are not having the review?

Count Down Days: Believe me I have been there, where I think I cannot go one more day only too realize that we have a break coming up and be so happy. While it is okay to start count down of 10 or so days as you close in on Christmas Break, Spring Break or before other holidays, if you are counting down all of the time and for extended time such as 179 to go, you are in the wrong profession. As a side note: Do not wish your life away. Life is too short anyway.

Only 179 days to go after today!

Can't Take Constructive Criticism: Hopefully you are  in a perpetual state of improving. If you think you are perfect and in no need of any kind of improvement, do us all a favor and get out of teaching now. Otherwise, open your ears and listen. Take constructive criticism and use it as a springboard to be ever improving your teaching. The teachers who hate their jobs are those who are unmoving. They will not change or bend wanting to keep everything just the same. Teaching is ever-changing just like everything else.

What do you mean you don't think my lesson is effective? I refuse to change. Effective this in your face…

D

Doing Personal Graduate Work in Class: This is a big no-no. Even though you have autonomy in the classroom, you need to be careful not to abuse your ability to make your own lessons. I have seen some teachers who are working on graduate studies use their students to research their graduate work. The students are not there to be your own personal unpaid interns. If you are pursuing a graduate degree, make sure that you have enough free time to do your work. You can use your classroom statistics as data when defending your thesis just don't use them to do your thesis. I knew a teacher who was being observed. The administrator noticed some students peeled off to the side working on what seemed to be a separate project. It turned out to be the teacher's thesis. Needless to say, the teacher was reprimanded. Do what you are paid to do. Teach.

Sorry class I have a big college project due this week. Get handouts. Oh and Tiffany you don't have to do the handouts. I need you to help me input this data.

But I thought you were going to help us with our Science Fair projects today.

Not today. You're on your own.

<u>Doesn't Show Up for Duty:</u> This is a pet peeve of mine. It seems that there are all kinds of teachers. But as for duty, I can put them into two categories. First, those who show up for duty. They realize that it is something they should do and they do it. They don't have to be reminded. They put it on their calendar and show up for the entire time. Second, is the teacher who feels like someone will always cover their duty or they are too good, too busy, too something to do what others have to do. Most of the time, these people are the same people who sign up to bring bread for the get together, but will tell everyone — sorry I forgot or something came up. This is irresponsible. During duty you can get to know students who aren't in your class, you can be a representative for the school, or give students their first welcome of the day. If you have duty — do the duty. Do it without prodding. Do not do it ONLY because you will get in trouble for not doing it. It is a part of your job. You are paid for a complete job. It would be just as if you decided that you weren't going to turn in your grades at the end of the 9 weeks. Do it because you are supposed to do it.

I haven't done duty in 4 years. I just don't show up.

And you are proud of that?

Dates Parents of Students:  This is a dangerous, slippery slope. The parents of your students can be really cute, but dating them can open a can of worms you might not want to open. Plus, it can put the student in a very precarious position if the relationship ends badly. My advice is if you find someone you can't live without and can't wait until the student is out of your class or you can't move the student to another teacher's classroom, please proceed with caution and keep it under wraps for as long as you can to help all involve cope. Of course, if the parent is married it is always a hard NO.

Your Dad is really cute.

Dates Students: The only thing I'll say about this is it is never okay. NEVER!!!

I mean I'm only 24 and even though he is only a junior, he is 18. That's not much difference. He's actually an adult.

<u>Doesn't Put In the Effort on Group Professional Projects</u>: This is another pet peeve of mine. The person who does not want to do their part of a teamwork project. The reason it was assigned to the group is for the group to do it. I have been in groups when the manipulation is "you can do it so much better than me." It doesn't really matter who can do whatever better. What does matter is all involved ARE involved in doing the work. There is nothing more disheartening than to do all of the work and have someone get up and present it and take the credit. That is the quickest way to get on the bad side of a colleague. Don't shirk off your responsibility. Do the work you are supposed to do.

> I have a date tonight. I trust you to do the project. Just let me know my part. I'm so glad we are on the same team.

<u>Dreamer—Encourages Dreaming</u>: I love this part of teaching. You get students at all stages of their development. You can choose to help them nurture their strengths. I had a student who was a prankster. He always wrote poems, raps. He became a successful rap artist later in his life. Just because the gifts the students display don't fit into your lesson for the day, don't discourage it. Try to steer the student into a different time or place (talent show, a separate free time in your class) to showcase their gifts. You can also bolster the budding activist by encouraging entrance into a speech contest or suggest the future doctor join the Science Club. You might be listening to a speech one day and hear your name mentioned as a catalyst to what they became. The biggest gift of all—a successful student reaching their full potential. There's nothing better.

> No dream is too big or too silly or too unattainable. Reach for the stars.

<u>Dresses Like the Students:</u> Even the youngest teachers should dress as professionals. This doesn't mean that on casual day you can't wear jeans and a T-shirt. It means that the cute little tops that all of the 14-year-olds are crazy about shouldn't be in your wardrobe for school. Be aware of the message you send. The students might see you as a peer, causing you to lose some of your credibility. You never want to lose that edge. Those cute shirts that make you look like a teenager, please wear them on your own time and not as part of your professional attire. You want there to be an invisible line of exactly who is the teacher and who is the student drawn all of the times.

Haley, I liked your shirt so I went to The Teen Store and got the exact same one.

<u>Drinking and Eating:</u> Addressed before, but it won't hurt to go over it twice. Please don't constantly eat and drink in the classroom. Students can't and it's unfair to them to see you eating and drinking. If you must have something to drink and food all of the time, please try to take your bites and your sips between classes, during meals, during planning or consider not being a teacher. There are many jobs that will allow you to constantly eat and drink at your desk.

Wait let me get a drink of coffee and eat a bite before I start teaching. Talk quietly for a few minutes.

# E

Elitist—Teaching is Not Good Enough for Them, Always Looking for a Better Job: I had an intern one time who always talked about the fact that she didn't want to be a teacher. She wanted to be an administrator. That was her goal. I don't mean to squash your hopes of advancing within the school system, but let me tell you that the best principals are those who experience teaching in the trenches first hand. Most districts make their teachers teach for so many years before being able to apply for assistant principals, etc. When you are interning or applying for your first job, don't constantly be talking about the next job you want. Make sure you get the first job first. Most hirers don't want to hire people who aren't "ALL IN" for the job. Be "ALL IN." Your students deserve a teacher who is "ALL IN."

Expectations: Too High or Too Low:  If you have to go low or high with expectations for yourself or students, please go high. Students will always attempt to rise to your expectations. Judge in increments. Soar for the best. If you have a project that you'd like the students to do, model an A+ project. If they don't achieve the top, make sure that you point out parts that exceeded your expectations and downplay those that didn't. One parent once said, "I don't know why my son doesn't behave. I tell him every day that he is awful. He acts just like his dad and will not amount to anything." I can tell you from experience if you tell a child daily something negative about himself, he will eventually believe it. He will live up to your low expectations. Do not tell students they are bad. They are not bad. Maybe a particular action will disappoint you, but choose to use it as a teaching moment. Tell them what you want them to do. Model how you want them to behave. Point out model behavior and always, always point out their positive attributes. And tell them constantly that they can do it.

You are the smartest students.

I don't think Johnny will ever be able to make better than a 'D.'

F

Fun: It is not wrong to have fun in your classroom. The best and most engaging lessons were the ones that not only taught a lesson, but also were fun. I only caution that you must make sure that your fun lesson is a controlled fun. Fun activities can get out of control quickly. In one of my lower special education school classes, we had a game that we would play to recognize money. The students loved this game. They would beg to play it. Before long it became the prize they would get on Fridays if they had behaved all week. I loved that I could incorporate learning, fun, and reward all into one activity. That rarely happens, but when it does it's great. Make sure that you find resources to incorporate teaching and fun. The internet has a wealth of knowledge, as well as teachers at your school, and other teachers in your district. Don't be afraid to join a site where teachers help other teachers. As a whole teachers are a sharing bunch which is great because we can all use help in finding engaging lessons.

Have you heard what we're doing in Mrs. Mathers class? So much fun.

Flirty: Be professional, no flirting on the job with anyone. It is never okay! NEVER!

Wow, Ms. Allison, you are looking fine today!

Oh, Principal Manley. You look so handsome in the color.

Favoritism: Students will notice if you favor one student over the rest. They are very perceptive. Be careful. Sometimes it helps to make a chart or put a check mark by the name of the student getting the special job. Make sure that you pass around that favorite activity. If your student likes to be the one to change the date on the calendar or close all the windows in the afternoon, make sure that you let all students who want that job get a chance EVEN if they aren't good at it. It's important to be fair.

> No, Sylvia, I want Josh to do that for me.

Fear of Making Mistakes: Teachers who always shirk responsibilities for fear of making mistakes are not good teachers. You must believe in yourself just as you believe in your students. You can be paralyzed by fear. Sometimes lessons are a risk. Sometimes they work and sometimes they don't. But the fun of trying something new is a risk. You will never grow unless you are willing to take a chance. Take a chance on yourself. Try different ways to teach, you might be surprised with the result. As a former teacher of student with special needs, I had to constantly be looking for new and different ways to get my material across. Don't teach afraid.

> I can't do that. What if it doesn't work?

> What if it DOES work?

Friends With Students: You have enough friends. I don't think this is ever okay. Avoid becoming friends with students until they graduate, then you can be friends with them. I would avoid being friends with them on social media also as this is a form of friendship, but that is up to you. I have just heard of teachers who have regretted their choice of letting students in on their social media life. Later, it might be uncomfortable to block, unfollow, unfriend, or drop them. Plus, parents might have something to say about teacher who follows their students. The way I handled this is to give a blanket response. I don't engage with students on social media until they graduate.

Ms. Pam is not sick. She just posted a picture of her with her family at the beach.

Fosters students: Once again, for those teachers who feel the need to take students home with them. I'm not trying to dissuade you from this, I'm only saying be very careful. I have known some teachers who get very involved with the family. I have known some students who parents ask the teacher for things way beyond his/her role. For example, one asked the teacher to get all of her child's birthday presents. The parent will sometimes think an invitation to THE student is extended to the student's parents, siblings, and extended family. All I am saying is proceed with caution and be able to back up when you need to. Fostering students is not part of the job description so don't let it interfere with your job as a teacher.

I'm exhausted. I invited my students, Joy and Latasha, over and they brought their siblings so I had five girls this weekend.

<u>Friends with Parents of Students:</u> This is a tight rope that you might not want to walk. If you do, proceed with caution. I go with the same advice of becoming friends with parents as with the students. Try to do this when they are no longer in your class or when they are no longer in school. This is trickier if you are already friends with the parents before the students enter your class. You can't stop being their friends just because their child is in your class. My suggestion, if possible, is tell the administrator or whoever is in charge of making up classes and see if there is a way to avoid this. Sometimes there is no way to sidestep this. You might be the only 9th grade algebra teacher and this student needs to take algebra. Just be aware and tread lightly.

I can't give Jay a 'C.' Our families are going to the beach together this weekend and I don't want to hear about it.

<u>Fast Eater:</u> A Big attribute of teachers. You only get 20-30 minutes to eat. To dismiss class, get food, sit, eat, throw away trash, get back to class, and possibly a bathroom visit. Not for the faint of heart. You learn to eat quickly.

Here's an apple for your lunch, Ms. Granger.

If only I had time to eat it...

Friends with Other Teachers: This is only a problem if you let it interfere with your teaching. Be aware. This can become a problem especially if one of your group is having a problem with the administration or another teacher. Be careful and don't be drawn into drama that has nothing to do with you. The other teacher's problems are not your problems. You can offer assistance, but be careful not to make their problems your problems. You are a separate entity and your job is your own. You should never let yourself get hooked up as a package deal as a professional teacher.

Flexibility: Be careful not to see all students as the same. Some students have access to computers and internet, others do not. Some students have lots of support at home, other do not. Some students have abuse or alcohol issues with caregivers they are dealing with, others do not. One size does not fit all. I can remember one particular student in high school who was pregnant. She came into the class pregnant. We did not know how she would finish her course work needed to graduate. It took a village. It took me, counselors, outside agencies to find the perfect answer for her. For her, it was on-line classes while she gave birth and stayed home for her set amount of time. We worked with her before she had the baby to make sure that she had the skills needed to be a successful on-line learner before she delivered. She took on-line courses to finish high school. This particular young lady went onto college. What works for one may not work for all, the trick is to care enough to find out what works. Believe me, sometimes it's not the first thing. You must be willing to try and fail and try, try again until you get it right. As frustrated as you are when a great plan doesn't work, you must be cognizant of how much harder it is for the student who is in the middle of trying to succeed.

Since we missed yesterday for the bad weather day and we had the bus issue this morning, we are going to do combine two lessons in one today. It'll be fun.

<u>Flexibility Part 2:</u> Another story I can share about flexibility is the planner who cannot change for anything. This is a real problem because I remember when I was going for National Board Certification you had to video yourself. I was in the middle of my lesson and the fire alarm rang. It blew my whole lesson, but I lined up the students. Then they announced it had inadvertently gone off. I submitted that tape. It was real. It showed my flexibility in stopping a lesson mid-stream and how to get back into the lesson. Sometimes you have to think on your feet. You have to be able to change. You have to recognize that this isn't working and have plan B. If I get nothing else across to you, always have a Plan B. It's better if you also have a plan C or D. I would suggest an emergency plan for your sanity. Sometimes you have those lessons that just don't work. They blow up in your face. Always have another option. It's important. Especially when you are starting out. Your reputation as a teacher is cemented quickly. While it can be changed, it becomes much harder later. And I can tell you from experience that a good or bad reputation will follow you throughout the county even if you move schools. Be flexible, but be smart.

How can I teach today? I always use a black marker and I only have a blue one.

<u>Figuring out Differentiated Ways for Students to Achieve their Goals:</u> It is important to make learning fun. You want the students to engage in their learning. School is not just about memorizing facts. School is not just about regurgitating answers. Learning is the act of processing information. In order to truly learn, the student must acitvely particpate in their learning. Some of my best lesson plans were outside the box. Making a wanted poster for Pony Boy and Johnny. Games that review facts. Many of these can be found on-line. Some of your students can help you to invent. For a creative teacher, this is a wonderful way to fill your need to create. I know that most of you are told what to teach and when to teach so it is up to you to figure out ways to infuse the creativity and fun into lessons. Figure out ways to engage students. Inspire them to want to learn, want to come to your class. One thing I always heard is that on the first day if you expect students to read out loud, to speak, or to participate in class, you must give them an nonthreatening way to do that and be successful at it first day. I had a non-reader and I had him read out loud on the first day. Granted, I fed him every word that first day, but eventually his reading improved. All it takes is success. Make sure that your classroom is a safe place. No bullying, no ridicule. Set those rules up first thing. Better yet let your non-readers read the rules. It's a way to start.

Let's make a social media page for every character in our book we are reading. Who are their friends? What do they like to do? What's important to them?

G

Gamer or obsessed with phone: This is for the teacher obsessed with gaming or are on their phone constantly. Whatever your obsession; on-line gaming, fantasy leagues, your phone, you have to be careful. Don't let your outside life bleed into your professional job. There might be some wiggle room on this type of activity in other jobs. I caution you at school. Restrict time on devices. You don't want a parent to come to a meeting and say that their child reported all you talked about in your classes is gaming and fantasy leagues or that you were on your phone all of the time.

I'm sorry just let me get to this next level then I'll pause the game and help you.

Gripes about Other Staff at School: People's alliances change, but teachers at a school do not always change. You need to be careful about making disparaging remarks about teachers or other staff members. You might not be aware of issues. A teacher might miss a lot and have confided to the administration that she is going through chemo, but decided it is not something that she wants to share with the entire faculty. A good rule of thumb is to follow your mother's advice. "If you don't have anything good to say about a person do not say anything." You also need to be careful about joining into conversations that go that way. You don't want to be drawn into drama. Moreover, unless you are a perfect person, it is not wise to judge others.

Principal Manley called another teacher meeting. Ugh! I can't stand Principal Manley. Can you?

Mr. Price's students are too loud.

Gossiper- Just stay away from gossip. Let's face it, a school is a hotbed of gossip. There is gossip about students, their parents, the teachers, the staff, etc. Of course, first and foremost, don't be a gossip. Try to stay away from those who gossip, like I said before if you don't have anything good to say don't say anything. Please don't spread stories. Gossip almost invariably gets back to the people who are being gossiped about. It can be hurtful. It's also a form of bullying. We all know that bullying is not allowed in school. I would say one of the parts of your job is to help make your working environment a pleasant place. Another cautionary tale. With student's easy access to phones, the mistakes in the halls and in the classroom have a big possibility of being recorded and spread all over the world. How awful would it be to see yourself on social media meanly gossiping about a fellow teacher?

H

Heart too Free: I know that you want all of the children in your charge to have all of the things they need and want, but please be careful about spending your own money. Your money will only go so far. Unfortunately just as you are always expected not to show favoritism in the classroom, if you don't spend the same amount of money for all children in your charge then you are in essence showing favoritism. I would suggest an alternative. Look for places that will support your students. Many programs are already set up and would be happy to supply students with paper and school supplies, including backpacks. Work with your counselors at your school to identify the resources. Numerous charities give out free food to needy families. There are also programs that fund and deliver supper and summer meals for students who are eligible for free lunch. Clothing and various other items such as holiday presents can also be acquired through funded programs. The bottom line is before you open your wallet, which is just a quick fix, do your research and facilitate change. Find a place for these families to tap into that will be a more long-term fix. Help by finding and sharing information so the student can get help.

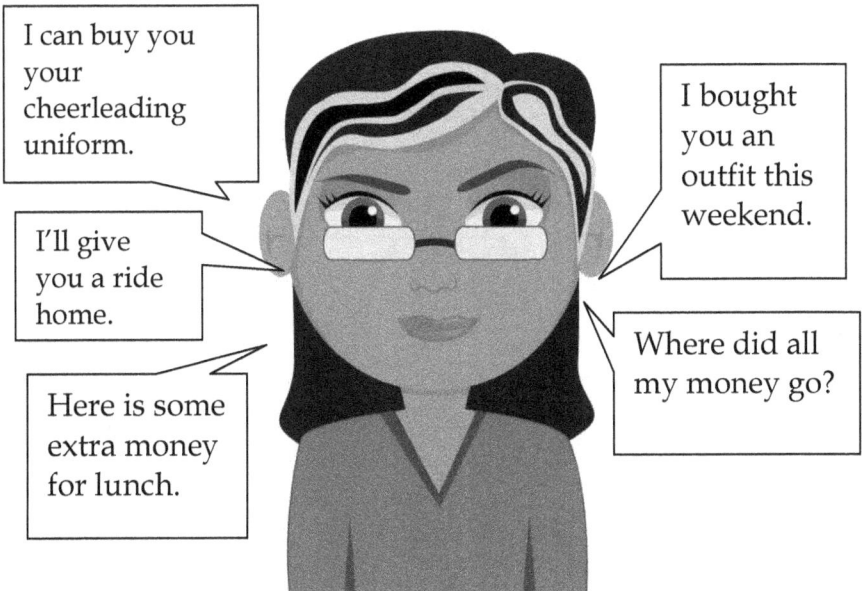

Hands Students the Answers: I consider this a real disservice to the students in your class. Let's face it, you either made the test or have the answer key so you know the answer. I have seen many teachers do this or allow the helper or the Teacher's Aide in their classroom to spoon feed the answers to the student on hand outs, homework, study sheet, even tests. This does not help the student. If the student doesn't learn how to find the answer on their own, then they are not learning. Just giving them the answer doesn't help anyone. It is just being a bad teacher. Teaching is an art. Learn your art. Hone your craft. If your student doesn't understand what you are teaching, then teach him another way. Students come in a variety of learners. Some are visual, while others are auditory, and still others use the kinesthetic learning styles. It is up to you as a teacher to figure out how your student learns. The only way to successfully figure out how individual students learn is by trial and error. The best teachers teach the same objectives in a variety of ways so each student can process it through all learning styles.

I don't have time to explain how you get the answer.

The answer to question 3 is 'B.'

Handout Queen or King: The most uninvolved type of teaching is the teacher who just uses handouts exclusively. You've seen them. You walk into the class and there is a set of handouts on the front table. The student is expected to pick up the handout, fill it out, and turn it in. If you are lucky, the teacher reviews the handouts at the end of the day. So what do some students do? They doodle until the end of class and just write down the answers when they are given. I've seen some teachers not even take up these handouts. At one point, I tried to help a new teacher making sure she met the new teacher requirements. She was responsible for passing a variety of tests, completing on-line courses, and self-actualization projects. About 3 weeks into her teaching, she came to me with a problem. Her students refused to do her work. I quizzed her and found that she assigned handouts daily. She said at first the students would complete them, but now they had stopped. I asked what she did with the handouts. She said she threw them in the trash. I explained the assignment needed a reward or consequence, a grade. As a side note, this teacher called later to tell me that she had gotten in trouble for leaving to get coffee during the day. She left her class unattended. No matter how much I tried to help her, she just did not get it. She did not last the year. Some people are just not teacher material and it's important to recognize that too.

Handouts are on the back table.

Hands-on Queen or King: This is one of the most positive attributes of a great teacher. I really like this style of teaching. Just don't overdo it. I think we all need a little of the hands-on queen or king in us. This teacher loves to teach through engaging her students. She is a project person, a center person, she is the person who figures out how to use the big game to teach math or how to use a news story to generate a lesson. This person is creative and always thinks outside the box. This teacher really understands differentiated instruction and is well aware of the three learning styles, auditory, visual and kinesthetic. There is a plethora of places to find hands-on activities for a variety of subjects. Use the internet, other teachers, teacher-made sites, etc. to gather ideas to make your class fun and engaging.

Today we are going to do our science experiment.

Class, line up. Each of you will represent a specific place value.

We are going to learn about fractions today while eating this pumpkin pie.

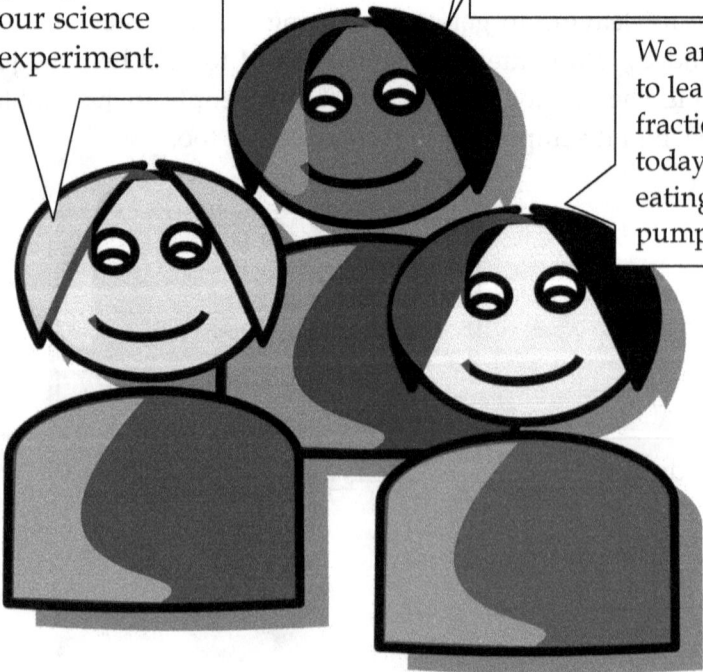

I

Interns as Personal Subs or Abuse of Interns: Teachers don't use your interns as your own personal unpaid assistants. There are three types of teacher who have interns. First, the one who gives their class to the intern pretty much from day one and is never in the classroom. This teacher reads magazines in the teacher's lounge for hours saying the intern is running her class. Granted, you are supposed to teach the intern to teach, but be there to guide them. You can leave them for short bursts of time but in reality, you need to be careful. If anything were to go wrong in the classroom, it ultimately comes back to you. Your classroom is still your responsibility. Second, the teacher who won't let her intern do anything. This teacher doesn't help the intern either because this teacher micromanages everything. How can the teacher learn if she is not able to at least take over some? Never reprimand your intern in front of your class. If it's that bad, make up an excuse, have the intern step outside, and correct her. Nothing ruins an intern quicker than being corrected in front of students. The last kind of teacher of interns is the kind you want to be. You guide the intern, let them take over the classes little by little. You listen to their suggestions and let them take the reins on planning and guiding lessons on their own. This way the intern learns. You make yourself available to guide and help them. Interning is a great way to learn to be a teacher. Help them achieve greatness. We need all the good teachers we can get.

I love having an intern. I don't have to do anything for the entire semester. My only problem this semester is being bored.

In-service Queen or King: These teachers are the ones who always want to plan in-services for everything. Granted there are some in-services that are helpful and needed to learn about things. But it is ridiculous to have in-services to train you on something that you don't even have and have no hopes of having. I've even gone to in-services to learn how to use a grading program and the district never even buys the program. Some of these in-services could be set up as an online tutorial and accomplished in half the time. The most powerful way to turn a teacher off to implementing a new program is an in-service that is poorly executed, obviously unneeded, it is for unavailable technology, or too long.

I'm presenting the in-service on the latest smart board. So excited!

But, we don't have the latest smart board. Why do we need to know how to use it?

It's Not My Fault: This is just a bad attribute to have all the way around. If you do something and get in trouble, own up to it, use it as a learning lesson for yourself. Don't try to wipe the blame on someone else. That only gets them in trouble and if it's not true then it ruins your credibility and colleagues lose trust in you. To be honest, if YOU can't be honest think about another line of work.

I only did that because Sarah suggested that I should do it this way. If you want to reprimand anyone, reprimand Sarah.

Inflexible: A pertinent part of being a good teacher in flexibility. You never know when that fire drill might ring or a student might throw up or a needed piece of media equipment will break down or act up. All of these are the reasons teachers must be able to think on their feet or have a Plan B. If you do nothing else in your pre planning days, figure out what you'll do if everything falls apart. You still have a classroom of students looking at you. Your back up could be reading material for uninterrupted reading. This will keep the students quiet while you work on whatever it is you need to work on to get your class back on track. Another idea is drawing. Most students have a piece of paper. Your first and best solution is to teach the lesson in a different way that side steps the problem. Examples: Change to a discussion, engage students in generating a list on the board, divide into groups and give the students the points you were going to make and have them research and teach it to the class. Have them open the book and practice. Have them come to the board, do, and show math problems. You have many ways to teach students. If your first way breaks down, you better be ready to keep the class going even if you have to think outside the box.

How can I possibly teach my lesson now? The smart board isn't working.

My class can't go out for the fire alarm, we haven't covered pages 11-25 yet.

<u>Instigates Fights with Other Teachers, Staff Members, Students,</u>
<u>Parents, etc.</u> Drama and keeping drama going keeps these teachers
going. There are teachers who will pass along information or set up
things to get staff or students to argue with each other I call these
types of teachers—Dramaholics. They are always looking for the
drama. There is no place for this in the classroom. I had a teacher
like this in my building one time. She would have conversations
with different teachers and then proceed to go to that teacher and
repeat the conversation peppering it with her dramatic twist.
Usually the Dramaholic repeats one piece of the conversation that
could be construed in a negative way. Be careful of anyone who
seems to maliciously talk about others. Be wary that they are just
looking to load up on negative talk that they can drop in the
subject's lap. A peaceful school is a good school. Don't look or
invent drama. Don't be a Dramaholic.

You should talk to Sue in building 3 she was talking about you this morning. I can't repeat what she said. It was awful. All I can say is I wouldn't take it. You should confront her.

Immune System: Teachers are exposed to all kinds of sicknesses. I can tell you that every time I moved from one school to another, I got sick. You need to be diligent about eating healthy, getting enough sleep, and taking care of yourself so you can keep a strong immune system. I know that you want to go to work even when you're sick, but think of the students. We don't want them at school coughing and sneezing all over everything. You shouldn't go to school when you know you're contagious. You must also be consistent with sending sick students home. A lot of times you are the one who notices if a student's eye is pink or if his face is flushed. There should be someone at your school designated to take a temperature or handle a mini triage in your front office or guidance area. A lot of elementary schools have nurses on staff, some do not. Find out what the rules are about where to send sick students and be diligent with keeping as much sickness out of your classroom as possible. Remind students about hand washing, talk about handwashing, and model hand washing. Hand washing is the best and easiest defense against contamination. Stay Healthy.

J

<u>Joiners:</u> These are teachers who join every committee or group project that comes their way. They usually don't serve in a leader capacity. They just want to attend the meetings and serve. There seem to be two types of these over-joiners. The ones who like the social aspect of the group interaction and those who want to be listed as members, but have no intention of serving in any real capacity. They just want to stuff their resumes. The first can hijack your meeting with social personal dribble that can cause the meetings to go way over time and the second serve no real purpose, but usually are less of a problem. Nonetheless, neither actually contributes, so beware of the over-joiner or beware of becoming an over-joiner. Make sure that you volunteer because you genuinely want to contribute.

What committee? I really don't care what it is. I'll be on that committee. Also, I want to serve as the senior board advisor.

<u>Jokester:</u> This teacher is a great social friend, and even though some levity in the classroom can make the classroom fun, be careful not to overdo it. Staff or students will not take you seriously if all you do is joke and pull pranks. You also have to be careful since pulling jokes and pranks can be a form of bullying. Make sure that this is not going on. Once a student hid a teacher's keys as a joke and the teacher ended up having to pay for the lost keys. When the student was caught, the teacher had to answer for allowing the student access to the keys. Bad all around. Pranks and jokes can also get out of hand or be taken the wrong way. Although it's fun to be fun. My advice is to not be too much of a jokester. Teaching students is a serious business.

Have you heard the one about...?

Let's hide the admin's notes so he can't find it when he gets back from the office.

# K

Keeps Constantly Searching for Other Jobs: There is nothing that will make students and staff lose respect for you more quickly than you always looking for another job. I have heard teachers gripe constantly about their job. Always looking for the bad part of it. This student did this, this teacher said this, the principal did this. You can find something bad in any situation. You should fully embrace the job you're in while you are in it. If teaching is just a place holder for something in your mind that is bigger and better, then you will not be effective at the job that you are in. You will be dissatisfied, always looking or something else and you'll lose the joy of teaching. Students will suffer, since you don't have your whole heart into it. Take a hard look at yourself. Are you really "in" this job or is this just a step along the way? If it's just a step, do us all a favor and get out of teaching.

Sorry, I can't help you with your lesson, I need to do research for a new job I'm interviewing for next week.

Know-It-All: This teacher knows everything. You can't dispute him, he will argue with you over the most minute point. He's exasperating for you and for his students. While it's great to have a great intellect and have information on many trivial things, it is also exhausting for the person on the other side of the conversation. I knew a teacher like this; he dominated out staff meetings. No one could get anything done because no one knew better than he did.

Let's stop the meeting and check me on that. I know I'm right. It was 2013 not 2014.

L

<u>Loves the Textbook, Won't Deviate:</u> This teacher goes hand in hand with the teacher who is inflexible. If you only teach from the book, you might miss the differentiated instructional ways that help students with various learning styles. If you only have the student look at the book and answer questions, then the auditory learner is getting left by the way side. Step out of your comfort zone and try something new. This is a form of insecurity to never deviate from the book. But beware too much deviation from what is expected of you can get you in trouble too.

I can't teach it that way, if it's not in the book, it's the wrong way.

<u>Loyalty—Too Much—Blind:</u> If something is bad, then say something. Go to your union representative, if you have one, or to a person in authority. Most districts have ways to bring problem issues to their attention without getting the person in trouble. Sometimes called a whistle blower or something else. Don't have blind loyalty. One district had a group of educators change answers on a standardized tests. If others were aware, then they should have reported the crime. Loyalty is great, just make sure it is deserved.

I knew it was wrong, but I wanted to be loyal. Now I'm in trouble too.

<u>Lack of Loyalty For the School You Work At:</u> If you're at a school, there is a certain amount of loyalty that is expected and should be given. So be careful as you talk to others that you don't sell your school down the river. If you see something that is being done better at another school then bring that different way back to your school. See if you can get the improvement implemented or at least a version of it implemented. Never be that person who trashes their school. Be proud of where you work.

> Let me tell you everything bad thing about my school. I never really liked working here anyway.

<u>Listener:</u> Teachers can talk with the best of them. But sometimes we just need to be good listeners. I had student write in a journal on a daily basis. My ongoing plan was to take the journals up on Friday, read them, and grade them. I never will forget the time that I read a particularly shy 9th grader's. I read this outpouring of pleas for help that had started Monday. It seems this girl was being abused and this was her way of telling me. Of course, I immediately got her help from the counselor and her situation was resolved. I definitely changed my practice. I told the students if they wrote something they needed me to read right then, to put it on my desk and not back on the folder table. That way I never had to read a heartbreaking situation like that again. Be good listeners.

> Can you believe the principal said that? Sorry, I wasn't listening what did you say?

> I said, the principal is standing behind you.

<u>Lesson Planner</u> — <u>Too much, Not Enough</u>: Believe me, we all need a plan. You try getting in front of 30+ students and winging it. It might work for one or two lessons, but eventually it'll catch up with you. You will be just spinning your wheels and you won't be an effective teacher. There is an art to teaching. Make sure you have a plan. I find it better to over plan. I'd rather have too much to do than not enough. You will master the knack of skipping or reducing what's left on your plan. I have known teachers who decide to work strictly from the textbook's plan, which is fine as long as you review that plan before you try to implement. You never know what might go wrong. By making plans and tweaking them each time you introduce the lesson, you are improving them. You should always review your plans after your class. Ask yourself: What worked? What didn't work? How can I improve this lesson?

Lesson Planner Part 2: Review media and resources before showing. Do NOT show media you find on the internet without a review first. You never know what might not be needed or what might be inappropriate for a certain age group. The last thing you want to is to have to develop a whole new lesson trying to explain or minimize the damage done by an unviewed lesson on media. Plus you can get fired for showing something inappropriate. You are supposed to review the resource, not just guess it will be okay because you found it on the internet. Be smart.

I can't wait to get home and tell mom about the curse words that were on the video clip that Ms. Rogers showed today. Mom won't let me watch anything like that. I need to tell her that the teacher thinks it okay.

Lives For School— No Outside Life: There are teachers that their jobs are their whole life. These teachers usually have no personal families (children, spouse) at home. But, sometimes they do. They allow the school be all-consuming. I had a department head one time who would place long drawn out hand written and copied ideas in our boxes early in the morning. We realized that she lived and breathed the school. Now while this is an admirable trait to a point, a person who is obsessed with something will sometimes expect those around them to be just as obsessed with the object of their obsession. Even if we wanted to implement the idea, she never stayed on it long enough to see if it worked before she had another idea that she claimed was the best thing ever. The problem is that you never fully implement anything.

Today, we're going to try the Poe Strategy. It was in your boxes this morning. I know that I just introduced my idea from last week. You can get rid of that now.

M

Meeting Just the Minimum Requirements: Teachers, you know the student who always does just enough to earn them a passing grade, the one who never tries to excel or improve. Don't be that teacher. Sometimes it's worth the little extra time planning, or talking to a student, or staying at a meeting. Make sure you are not counting down. I knew a teacher one time who would start walking slowly to her car 10 minutes before regulation end of the work day so she would arrive at her car precisely one minute before time to go so she could drive out right on time. Don't be that person, put in the time needed to do the job. Make sure you plan those lessons, especially starting out or starting something new. As you get more and more experienced, you can reuse lessons. The first year is always the hardest, but don't skimp on time. I am not advocating living at school. Just make sure you don't get so caught up on putting in your exact hours that you forget what you are hired for- to teach. Stay a few minutes more to finish or prepare. It'll pay off with success.

Sorry, we're in the middle of the problem. But my day ends in 5 minutes. I'm outta here…4,3,2,1…Bye!

<u>Mistakes Not Owned Up To:</u> Don't always slough off your errors as someone else's problem. If this type of teacher spent as much time fixing the problem as they do blaming everyone else, life would be a lot easier and they would be a better teacher.

> It wasn't my fault. It was a computer error.

> Oh…we didn't use the computer. It doesn't matter because I know is it wasn't my fault.

<u>Making Students Accountable:</u> Students might come with all kinds of excuses as to why they can't do the assigned work. You have to make them accountable. You have to teach them time management. One of the greatest things you can teach students for future is a real world concept—time management. Part of the project should be a list of what should be completed and when. Set a timeline for the student. Tell them exactly what is due and when. Make sure that they don't get behind. If you start this early, when they are in college they will thank you. Have them make lists, use technology to keep up. Remember a lot of what you teach them in terms of managing time will carry forward into the real world.

> I know I had six weeks to finish, but I just started it last night. This was the best I could do.

<u>Meeting the Parents, Good or Bad:</u> Meeting the parents is always tricky. If you will keep this one thing in mind, you and the parents should be on the same page. You both want the student to be successful. Start off with that. You do not want to come off as the enemy or the person out to make their child's life or the parent's life more difficult. Keep the parent looking at the end result. If your child is successful in school, chances are he will be successful in life and that is in fact the ultimate goal. There are some problem parents. I had a parent come for a teacher meeting one time and I explained that the student was failing because he had not turned in the assignments. In the meeting, the parent slapped the student and started yelling at him. This was unacceptable and we told her so. It gives you a whole new perspective on the student. While you can't tell a parent how to parent, there are rules to be followed in school and not hitting is one of those. I found a different way to help the student become successful without involving the parent. I also had a special education student who acted up in school. After I told the parent, the student came in with black and blue marks. After referring the matter to the counselor, I found a different way to help the student without involving the parent. Be aware of the parent who will blame you for everything. It becomes an 'us' against 'them' type thing. These are extreme cases and for the most part, parents want to help their child to succeed. Work as a team, since both you and the parents should all be on the same page.

Hello, I'm Kevin's Mom. Nice to meet you.

I'm one of Kevin's teachers. I'm going to go over some strategies that I hope will help Kevin do better in my class.

Glad you are here. But there' no hope for Kevin. He's a horrible student.

<u>Making Fun:</u> This is a type of bullying that should not be tolerated and certainly should not be modeled. There are two types. Those who are constantly trying to find the good in people and those who are constantly trying to find what is negative, always cutting people down. Don't be the second kind of teacher. Be careful about what you say about fellow teachers and staff members and especially students. And don't tolerate that type of behavior in your classroom. If you don't allow it, it won't happen. I've heard of student's being shamed just for her name pronounced Fe-mall-lee. It was spelled female. She didn't name herself. Other examples are: the large boy, the one with a lisp, the boy who stuttered, the girl who developed early, the immature student, the struggling student, or the student living in poverty. Shaming is so prevalent in our society today that we have to be careful with these young and very vulnerable psyches. Students are sometimes constantly bombarded with social media messages of public shaming. There are too many stories about suicides and other horror stories about what goes on outside of the classroom. Make your classroom a safe place. Make sure that you always pick out the positive traits and build students up; it might be the only nice thing they hear all day. Sometimes teaching is more than just English and math.

Monitoring Students So They Can Reach Full Potential: You have a great opportunity to watch and guide your students. Make sure that if they have a gift you encourage that gift. If you see a student who doodles and they are good, you might see a potential artist. Steer that student toward graphic art or sketch artistry. Help them explore career paths that will incorporate that gift. If they are exploring that gift on their own, it could be their passion. And as you know the best teachers are those who are passionate about their work. The most successful people in life are those who are the most passionate about their chosen field. Nurture that. Help them to find their passionate path.

N

<u>No Rules</u>:  Be consistent with discipline! Making sure that you follow your own rules and the rules of the school, is one of the musts of being a schoolteacher. If you are not consistent with your rules, then students can't follow them. They will assume that anything goes and if you've ever been in this situation you know if you give them an inch they'll take a mile. Don't get in this situation. I remember a young teacher who thought he could be friends with his students by always bending the rules. For example, if he was supposed to take his students to an assembly, lunch, or if they needed to be released at a certain time, this teacher didn't feel like those rules applied to him or his students. What resulted was a mess because to get to an assembly in an organized fashion, everyone needs to follow the time schedule. Otherwise, classes are sitting out of order and the assembly does not begin or stop on time. That one act disrupts. The same goes if they don't come to lunch on time. The last thing about not letting students out on bell is being disrespectful to the next class. The next class's teacher is expecting to be able to start her class on time. If the first teacher keeps students too late, it disrupts everything. Be respectful. There is a reason for the rules.

I'm sure the rules are just a suggestion, not hard and fast. I don't need to follow them. I'm a free spirit.

No to Everything: Although there are definitely times that no should be the answer. Make sure that your answer is not always no. Take a look at yourself and see if this is you. Students will quit coming to you for help. Teachers will quit coming to you for collaboration. You will be an island and we all know that a teacher can't be an island.

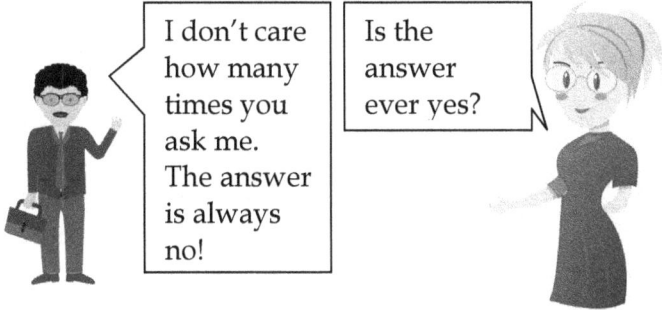

> I don't care how many times you ask me. The answer is always no!

> Is the answer ever yes?

Nice: You can never be too nice unless you are always being taken advantage of. Try to be aware, but I say that I'd rather be a little taken advantage of and be nice than not be nice. You have to draw the line. The best way to do this is size up those on your team. If you see that one of your team members is always putting stuff off on you, you make the choice. Are they doing it because you are absolutely the best at what you do and you love doing it? Or are they taking advantage of you? When you answer that question, adapt your actions and reactions accordingly. Also make sure you don't take on too much because it is better to do a few things well rather than a lot of things in a mediocre way.

> You are the best!

Novelty: Doing something new and different is always exciting. The only caution with this teacher trait is to make sure that if you do try new and different ways or teaching, do it sparingly and not every time. Infuse it in spurts. You can be spontaneous. In addition, what works for one teacher may not work for you. Remember if the lesson doesn't work in first period, you might need to change it or abandon it completely for the rest of the periods in the day. Don't try to adopt someone else's way, be true to your personality.

I just saw this idea for a lesson this morning on the web and I thought I'd try it in the classroom today.

New: Just because something is new does not always make it better. If you are new to the classroom, you might want to make sure that you use some tried and true methods as you are getting used to the classroom. Wait until you feel secure and comfortable with your class to try something new.

This is something new. Teaching math through outdoor activities. I'm not sure about it. Plus, I'm not very outdoorsy.

<u>Next- always trying to do the next thing for students to learn:</u>

This is one of my favorite attributes of teacher. They always break down the steps, scaffold as they go, and review to make sure step one is completely understood before moving onto step 2. This is done through differentiated instruction and scaffolding to build on understanding. Presenting the problem first before showing the path to the solution by combining actions, images, and language. You must present material in a variety of ways to make sure that all learning styles are represented. You must make sure that appropriate time for practice and review are incorporated to make sure that actual learning is going on. This type of teaching will help your students and make your job so much easier.

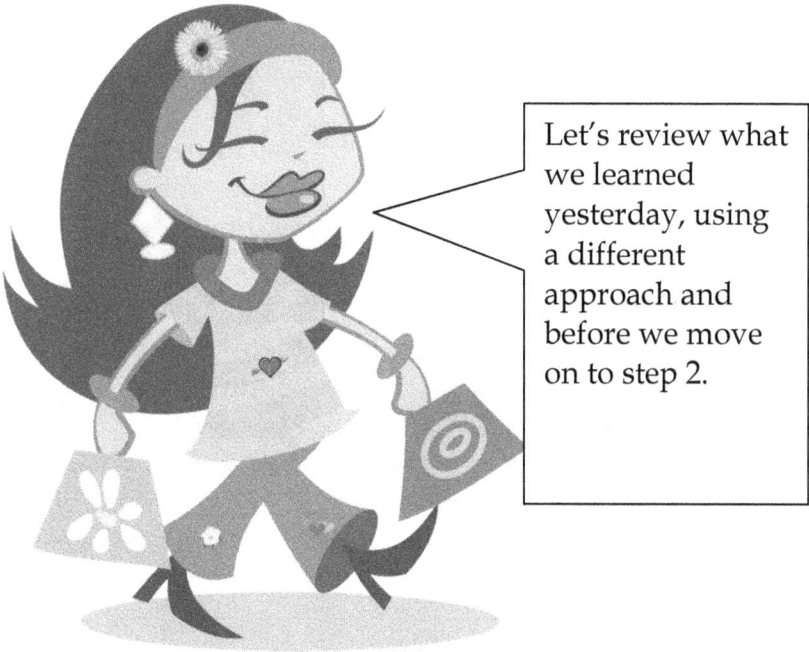

Let's review what we learned yesterday, using a different approach and before we move on to step 2.

O

Organizer: All teachers need to be somewhat of an organizer. We need to be able to organize our lessons, plan our lessons, and manage our time. But you need to be careful not to organize your way right out of teaching. You have to find some sort of flexibility in organization. There are times that an unknown surprise messes up your perfectly organized lesson. If you are unmoving, you will have a problem. I think it is better to over-organize. I do this even in my personal life. I make lists daily of what I need to accomplish. Organized people can keep school meeting times, parent meetings times, put their grades in, and turn their lesson plans in on time. If you have problems organizing, then take this time to try to make an organizational protocol that will work for you. My list making may not work for you, but figure out what does.

My list is finished. I've turned in my grades and made lessons for the week. Now if only I could make a list that would make Johnny get to my class on time tomorrow.

Over Sharer: There is a time and a place to share. You've heard the old saying TMI—too much information. Sometimes your weekend exploits need to stay just between you and your boyfriend. I never will forget the girl who shared that she had gotten so drunk the Saturday before that she had relieved herself in her bed. I could have gone my whole life without hearing about that. The people in your school do not need to know every horrid detail. This also goes for your students. They don't need to hear the gory details about your trip to the emergency room and all of the nasty things that you threw up in your toilet. Try to place yourself on the other side of that conversation. The work place is the work place so keep it sacred. Be professional.

Did you see my social media? I put everything that happened this weekend with pictures.

Yes, I heard about it from the principal.

The principal saw it? Ut-oh!

P

Phone Fetish: To me unless you have an emergency, you should not use your phones during class. We asked that the students put up phones in the class. Shouldn't we also follow our own rules? Your school has a main line so if something is an actual emergency, the office can reach you. Please refrain from using your phone during class. If you must, at least save use for change of class, breaks, planning, and other times when you aren't supposed to be teaching students.

Sorry class, I need to take this call. It's my boyfriend calling about our dinner plans.

Planner—Too Much or Not Enough: Plans are guides. They are not going to be published or at least most are not going to be published. Plans are a guide for you to follow to keep you on track and to make sure that you are teaching your students what they need to know. Most schools now adhere to strict guidelines of what needs to be taught at different grades and different levels using students' own personal levels of achievement to guide them. Just make sure that you leave time to actually teach. Just because you can write fantastic lesson plans does not mean that you can teach and vice versa just because you are a great teacher does not mean that everyone can understand your lesson plans. Find a happy medium.

My lesson plans for the week are 43 pages long. I'm too exhausted to teach them.

Prom: Prom- an example of trying to relive their high school days. I remember chaperoning the senior prom one year. One of the teachers, a male, was having his picture taken with all of the students. I was positioned at the entrance to direct the young couples or singles or groups toward the photographer, but this teacher had his camera and wanted his picture with all of the students. He would insert himself into their group as if he were still in high school. He was smiling and laughing and at a break I took the opportunity to ask a question. "Are you having fun?" He replied, "This is why I'm a senior class sponsor because I love all of the trips and prom and various other activities that the seniors are involved in." I noticed that he always chose to have pictures taken with the most popular students. You know the ones: the cheerleader, the quarterback, the valedictorian, the president of the student council. He seemed especially interested in the jocks and the cheerleaders. I asked, "Why do you want these pictures? Are you especially close these particular students?" He answered very honestly. "When I was in high school I was one of the forgotten. I never went to prom. I never got to experience being one of the popular crowd, but I always envied those people. But now look at me; I'm one of the popular people." I couldn't help but notice what he hadn't noticed that he was a good ten to fifteen years older than these students in his charge. Now I know and you know that the last thing these prom-going students wanted to do was to hang out and have their pictures taken with the older science teacher. But because he was in authority, none of them balked at the request.

Do you like my prom dress?

At 35, you might be a little old for a prom dress. You're supposed to be a chaperone, not going to the prom.

<u>Prom Part 2:</u>  So I ask you as teachers, remember who is in your charge. Most will not go against you. They want you to like them. They want whatever will give them an advantage in your world, something that could possibly give them the edge on rounding that grade of a 'B' up to an 'A' so be careful that you don't abuse your power as a teacher. You had your chance at prom, this time it is their time. Let them have these experiences unencumbered by your insecurities or desires to recapture a portion of your youth. Some teachers loved their school experience and they never wanted to leave it. The students need a teacher, not a friend. Don't become a teacher to relive your school days or to rewrite history. Become a teacher to teach.

Science teacher by day, crazy dancer at prom! I don't want to be no stinkin' chaperone.

Procrastinator: Teachers who procrastinate not only don't get their work done in a timely manner, they also model undesirable behavior for their students. Deadlines are present in all jobs, including teaching. Specifically, lesson plans must be turned in on time as well as teacher's portions of important group projects such as the recertification of their school. The last thing a teacher wants to do is to be completing paperwork or research at the last minute during their class because they procrastinated. Procrastinator's work is usually frenzied and incomplete. Don't be a procrastinator.

We need to finish the report.

I didn't get to my part, ran out of time.

I can guess at the statistics. I'll write it down. Give me a minute.

Did anyone do their part?

Promiser — Makes Promises and Keeps Them: This attribute goes hand in hand with consistency. If you make a promise to a student, then keep it. This also goes for promises made to administrators, staff, and other teachers. It's really a trust thing. If you have problems keeping promises, because you are a procrastinator or a poor time manager, then refrain from making promises. It's much worse to break a promise, than it is to just not make a promise. If you are constantly unable to keep your promises, practice the phrase "I can't promise you, but I will try."

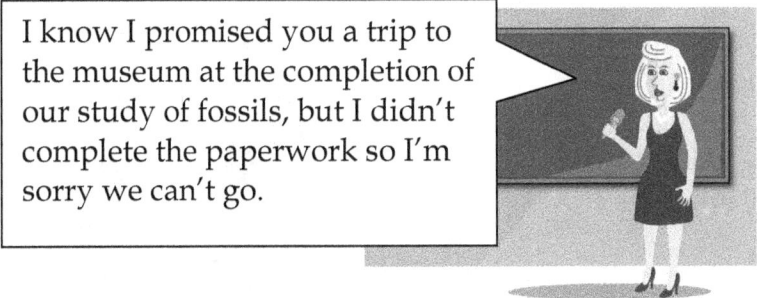

I know I promised you a trip to the museum at the completion of our study of fossils, but I didn't complete the paperwork so I'm sorry we can't go.

Q

Questions that Make Students Think: The best teachers are provocative in their quest for the student's learning. They're always asking open ended questions. They want the students to come to their own conclusions. They want them to question. It's important as we go through life that we ask questions. What is the purpose? How can this help me? What do you expect me to learn? How am I going to learn? What am I going to learn? Questioning can begin in the classroom, but it is hoped that it will carry on throughout life. The best students are the ones who question and search for the answers with your help. You are the facilitator of your student's minds. Nurture them.

I guess the question would be –Why is a cat teaching this class?

That's a lot of research for the question—What do you think we are going to have for lunch?

Questions Their Choice of becoming a Teacher: Don't go into teaching if you really aren't passionate about it. I have news for you teaching is not that lucrative of a profession so if you are in it for the money, you are in the wrong profession. If your passion is something else, then pursue that. Don't go into teaching as a place holder for something else. I can tell you there are a number of people who almost act embarrassed about being a teacher. Teachers who are parents say to me and others, "I would never want my children to be a teacher." Respect the profession and don't muddy our waters by being in a profession that you clearly should not be pursuing and one in which you clearly do not belong. Teaching is a noble profession and should be respected in every way.

My dream is to be a writer. I hate being a teacher, but it pays my bills while I pursue what I really want to do. I've been writing my great novel for 40 years now.

R

<u>Relieves High School:</u> Teachers, you have already had your school days. That time is over. Be a teacher to help your students learn and be successful during their school days, not because you want to relive your own glory days. The past is in the past, you can't get it back.

I was the captain of my cheer squad in high school. Maybe, I'll come and practice with your squad.

<u>Rules — Too Many:</u> There is a saturation point with the amount of rules. Make sure that you have only what you need. Try to consolidate. One rule can mean many things. Take the rule that simply states — Respect other. This should take in interrupting, making fun of others, bullying, taking turns, leaving others' property alone, etc. Rules should be listed, discussed, and explained in the first days of school. I am a big believer in posting these rules and referring to them often. I also believe that you should let your students engage and be involved in making the rules. If a student said there should be no bullying, then you can say we will list that as respect others. The explanation makes it all encompassing. It is a way to give the students ownership.

Students, check yourself. Read Rule #342.

Refuses to Teach What They Are Supposed To Teach—Too Free: Although things happen in the news that you might want to discuss, remember that you are a teacher and a teacher hired to teach a certain subject. Be careful when you stray off topic. Students will invariably want you to stray off topic. It's less restricting and demanding for them. Also, they might get out of daily work or homework. Beware of getting off topic. If there has been a lock down at school, then maybe a discussion about the what and why of the lockdown would be warranted. But random things in the news should be saved for those classes in which current events is the topic. Plus, it is too easy to insert your personal opinion into current topics. A Big NO-NO for teachers. You have a job to do and a specific amount of time in which to accomplish that job. You make lesson plans for a reason.

I know I should be teaching negative and positive integers, but I feel like talking about this editorial in the newspaper. I'm outraged!

Recognizing Teachable Moments: Teachers, one of the greatest moments in a classroom is when you teach a concept and the 'light' goes off for your students. Another wonderful moment is when there is a teachable moment that you didn't expect. Many lessons take a detour when a question is asked, or something extra is noticed, or a conclusion or theory is explored that was not anticipated. These are teachable moments. Some of these moments may be in the area of social interaction. As a teacher, you have the perfect opportunity and you have an obligation to not only teach the educational concepts, but to teach how to manage in 'real life.' Student need exposure to real life learning like how to get along with peers. Your classroom is one of the first places the students can watch how to get along with peers positively. Don't miss a chance to model good behavior, to point out appropriate reactions to others, and to discuss better ways to act or react. Recognizing teachable moments is a great attribute for a teacher to have. Strive to be that teacher who notices and capitalizes on those moments.

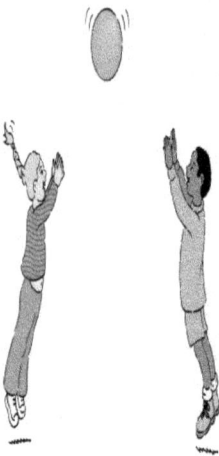

<u>Records Grades Keeps Good Data Records:</u> Almost all colleges and post high school situations ask for some sort of test scores to enter, so don't feel as if these students shouldn't practice taking tests. Don't go overboard and not teach the concepts. Don't teach only for the tests. Make sure you have hard data to back up the grades you give the students. You need to state in writing before your class starts your grading procedures. What percentage does participation in discussions count, quizzes, chapter tests, journal, homework, etc. These should all be listed and percentages known up front. If you do not have these specifics, then if a student disputes a grade, you will not have the data you need. It is very important that the grade reflects what the student knows. If you have a class that has all 'A's' and then they all bomb the standardized tests, you probably won't be a teacher very long. It is an unfortunate part of our school society. Students need to perform well on standardized tests to move forward with their education and the only way for them to have the ability to score highly is to know the material. So, testing and grades are a part of your life. Get used to it.

I'm giving Johnny a 'C' He seems average. But Gloria, I'm giving her an 'A' because she helps me every day.

Running into Students Outside of Class—Flipping Out: For the most part, teachers live in the community in which they work. They run into their students. I have seen students in a store, at the fair, at church, at the movies, and various other places. It is jolting sometimes at first because you see each other in a different context. It is good to be cordial to parents. Make sure that you don't get into a teacher conference out in the community. If that seems to be happening, steer that conversation away from the topic and suggest a meeting at the school. Downplay any problems with the student and make sure that you say something positive about their child. This type of interaction cannot be avoided. Be aware of the way you dress outside of class. Don't embarrass yourself. Remember your students are not the only people you might see. Your principal, people from the school district, and others who are in an authority position might be in the same place you are. You have to keep that in mind when teaching.

It was strange to see Mr. Rogers in his superhero costume at the grocery store. I didn't even know they had a comic festival this weekend.

# S

<u>See Something, Say Something:</u> Encourage your students to tell you about anything that happens in or out of the classroom that makes them uncomfortable or doesn't seem right. This goes for harassment of any kind or violent tendencies. In this day and time, it's important to help all students. Also, if you notice a student has a change in behavior or is journaling or creating artwork about harassment or violence, have a talk with that student during student free time if you feel comfortable enough to do that. Or if not, report the incident to a counselor or resource officer at your school. You see these students daily. You need to report a change in behavior. I have had a couple of student's behavior change as a result of a divorce or death in the family. One time a student was having a lot of problems and come to find out her family was homeless and living out of their car. Not a good situation or two teenage girls. You cannot stop everything, but you don't want to be on the other side of a tragedy and hearing everyone say, "We all knew." If you know, say something.

In Joy's journal today, she wrote about her mother's drinking problem. I'm going to refer her to the counselor to see if I can get her into a support group.

Social Butterfly: It's great to have celebrations, but be careful not to saturate the group. Two birthday cakes within two days is too much. You should have celebrations, but try to incorporate them into faculty meetings or department meetings as added extra of a scheduled meeting or get together. Remember, just because you have funds and time to make or buy a cake every couple of days don't expect everyone to have those sort of extra funds. Don't take up money for every little thing that comes along. I have been at school where they took up money so many times for this and that that I ended up having to say no. I ran out of money. Don't be afraid to say no. It is a voluntary fund and while I'm on the subject just because Vanessa gave $10 does not mean that you have to give $10. Be careful of this. Don't let the social aspect of your job overshadow your job.

I need $5 from each of you to buy a cake for George.

I just gave $10 for Brooke's cake yesterday.

Spends Group's Money Unwisely or Keeps Inaccurate Records: Collecting money from students is one instance where you have to be completely up front and keep meticulous records. The parents will come back and ask you where their money went. Always give receipts and make sure whatever you collect for is what you spend the money on. I had a parent tell me one time that she gave money for cheerleading track suits, but the track suits were never delivered. When approached, the sponsor said the money was not there. The sponsor was terminated the next year and that money was lost. It's important to spend the money on what you say you will. That teacher lost her job because she did not keep accurate records and did not manage the money appropriately. Who knows where the money went? But even though it is more than likely that the money was spent on some aspect of the cheerleading costs, it could not be determined. When you have many parents fussing about not getting goods for money given, then you lose your job. The sad thing is that she was a good teacher and a good coach to the girls, but she was not a good money manager. So let this be another cautionary tale.

<u>Sports Fanatic:</u> Even though as teachers, we may wear a variety of hats. It is important to keep those hats separate. So if you are the department head and a teacher. While in your classroom, actively teach. Do your department head business, answering emails, budgeting for supplies, making agendas for meetings, etc. during your student free time. If you have an extracurricular responsibility, make sure this does not bleed into your classroom. You don't want the administrator walking into your classroom when you are discussing strategy for the football game for the next week and your class is not working on your lesson plan. Just as you would not want a parent to call the school and tell the administration that students don't learn math, they talk about football. Remember to separate your jobs at the school and conduct those said jobs at the appropriate times and for the appropriate audience.

Let's put off that lesson on Physics again, I need ideas for the game plan this weekend. Anybody got any new plays you want to run by me?

Shares Lessons: The great thing about teachers is that they are sharers. Most teachers are only too happy to share successful lessons with you. The only bad thing would be if you used the exact same lesson on the same set of students and you were the first to see the students. But as long as students only take classes one time, which they should be, this should not be a problem. You are not expected to invent the wheel. Use and adapt what others have used and found success with. The bottom line is that all teachers want their students to grasp the lesson objectives, learn, and be able to implement and use the taught concepts. We accomplish this anyway that we can. So share. The only rule is to ask upfront, tell in advance, and give credit where credit is due. If you borrow a lesson from Mr. Redman, then say you got it from Mr. Redman. Teachers as a whole are not a selfish group.

I saw Mrs. Joiner implement this English lesson last week. We are going to try it today.

Statistic Follower: Statistics are to be used as guides to help with deciding about what strategies to use with instruction or on who to move forward or give extra attention. Don't sell your student's potential short. If you teach at a school listed as a low performing school, don't despair. Remember that is what happened last year, don't let that dissuade you. I am a big believer that students will work up to what you expect, so keep the statistics on the back burner. Don't let those statistics inform your every move. Don't expect less. Alternately, if your school always performs well statistically, you still have to keep up the same high expectations. Sometimes it is even harder to keep the higher level up because they are so high already that there is little room for improvement. Expect the BEST!!

100% of you will learn this concept today.

Strict Too Much, Not Enough: Leave a little wiggle room in your plans and how you interact with the students. Teach those things that are really important. If you want their name in a certain way and a student forgets, cut them some slack. I know it's important to follow directions, but if they have worked hard on an assignment and it is not even looked at because of a wrong name placement and given a zero; that seems unfair. Maybe a mark off? This segues into the discussion of failing and a zero. Teachers need to realize that the zero grade should only be given if a student has not turned in anything. As we all know, the zero averaged in is much more damaging that the 50 or 59 failing grade. So be aware of that. Don't be unmoving. On the flip side of that, don't be too loose. I've seen teachers assign a one page report with no clear instruction on font size or paragraph style. You might get four sentences from some students that fill up the page. Be specific with what you want. It's important. Don't be too rigid or too loose. Find a happy medium.

You get a zero because you did not write your name last name first.

Sends Out Students Constantly: Be careful about sending students out all of the time. There are some teachers who always want certain students out of their classroom. You're responsible for teaching all students. I know sometimes you get that student that you feel you can't handle. Maybe you just don't like them. I mean teachers are human too, but it is your job. You might have a job one day where there is a coworker that you can't stand. Remember that classmate in your school that you couldn't stand, you still had to deal with them. The best way to approach this is to look for something in which you can find common ground. I had a class one time in which there were all boys and this one girl. It was a middle school class. The boys behaved poorly in that class. I asked myself, "How am I ever going to get through this?" I realize after a couple of classes that the boys were all trying to get the girl's attention. So instead of trying to control the boys, I pulled the girl on my side. I took her in the hall and said all of these boys think you are so wonderful that they all want your attention, but I need to teach. I said if she could pay more attention, they might follow her. It worked. The minute the boys started acting up she told them that she wanted to listen to me. No longer getting positive attention for misbehaving the boys straightened up and I had a nice class for the rest of the year. This might not work in all classes. But my point is to think out of the box to make your class work and try to keep students in class if at all possible.

<u>Sponsor:</u> Don't be afraid to sponsor clubs or extracurricular activities. I know it's a lot of work and time, but the students appreciate it so much. A plus is that sometimes you get great trips or other perks. So keep an open-mind. But also go in with open eyes about how much time it will take. If you have responsibilities at home such as young children or an elderly parent, you might need to choose the less time demanding activities.

I'm going to Europe for the senior class trip this spring.

<u>Steals Money From Kitty:</u> Not much to say about this. Don't do it. Be honest. Even though some monies are gathered on such a low scale that they might not be audited, remember what the money was supposed to be used for. Don't use the collected monies for anything other than its stated purpose. It's never okay to take money that is not yours. NEVER!

I need to a couple of dollars for lunch. Here's the lab fund. No one will miss it.

T

Technology Lover or Hater: Technology is a wonderful thing. It's great to help explain lessons and as an addition to lessons. Technology can be under utilized and over utilized. Don't rely too heavily on technology-based lessons, but don't ignore them. Students are living in a technologically enriched world. You can't ignore it. Embrace it. And if you run into trouble with actually making the technology work. Just ask the student. They most likely know more that you do.

I've developed 13 lessons from recording our class as I taught Shakespeare. Here is number 1.

Takes Credit for Everything: You can't possibly have every idea. Only take credit for the ones you actually thought of and absolutely under no circumstances take credit for others' ideas. Plus, if you take credit for others' ideas, then they will know even if no one else does. At least, one person in the school will know you are a liar and to be honest one person is one person too many. It is Never okay to take credit for others' work. NEVER!

I pitched my idea to the principal and she loved it.

Great!

But, that was my idea.

Tester: I understand that we are in a standardized test world, but you have to be careful and not just teach to the tests. Your job is to make those students ready for the world. They need to graduate from school with the information and basic knowledge about math, social studies, history, English, etc. and to be able to tackle the world head-on. It doesn't matter if they are headed to college, the military, vocational school, or straight to a job. The curriculum that has been deemed important for those students to know before they get out of high school must be taught and taught in such a way that the student learns and retains the material. They should be able to use this information as they pursue their next step. Don't cheat these students by trying to short cut your way through it by just teaching them the test. A student who can pass a standardized test might be great at taking tests, but are they ready to tackle the world? Don't try to inflate test scores to help them look good on paper or to help you look good on paper. Either way, the paper wins and the student loses.

Today instead of learning how to calculate the answers, we will practice how to guess answers effectively on the standardized tests.

True to Your Personality: Of the many interns I have had, the biggest lesson I could teach them was to be true to your personality. I know you've heard to be tough and hard on students. This is true, but you really can't go against your personality. If you aren't a loud and hard person then it will go against your nature to try to be that in your classroom. You can adhere to the rules and make your class adhere to the rules and still be true to yourself. Instead of getting loud or yelling, quietly discipline if quiet is who you are. There are many varied negative discipline avenues for you to take. You can assign a time out, assign detention, stay in from outside play, miss a reward, or write the student up. But I think the most effective discipline is in the reward. Reward good behavior. I had an intern who tried so hard to be a yeller to get the students to behave and it just didn't work for her. She was a more passive person. The students didn't respond because it wasn't coming from her true self. If you decide to be a teacher for a career, you cannot keep up a mode in the classroom that is against your nature. Be true to yourself and find out what works for you.

We didn't get anything done in math today, Mrs. Mitchell spent the day yelling.

She is so sweet and soft spoken in Student Council meetings.

**Trip Hoarder:** There are some perks to sponsoring some activities and club or classes. Make sure that you don't sponsor just for the trips. I have known some teachers who don't do a lot of the work as a sponsor, but always seem to be on the list for a great free trip. Those teachers are the ones who when it's time to chaperone — the main reason for them being on the trip, they are no where to be found. Don't be this teacher.

> I'll sponsor the eighth grade class. I want to go on that trip to the theme park this spring.

**Too Laid Back:** While going outside on a beautiful day might work every once in a while to shake things up, just make sure that you are doing your job. I knew a teacher who hated being in the classroom so he took his class outside every pretty day. The act of going outside and coming back inside took valuable time off teaching. With ice breakers, review, new concepts, and working in time for practice; you can't possibly have time for this on a daily basis. So if you are assigned a classroom, you should use it. This same teacher had a parent come to sign her child out for a doctor's appointment and they could not find the student so the student missed their appointment. There is a reason you are assigned a classroom. If you want a job outside — seek recertification to become a teacher who spends most of their time outside or find a profession that you can be outside.

> I don't feel like teaching today, let's go outside.

Teaches own Kids: If you teach your own children, make sure that you are not too hard or too easy on them. It is not only hard for you, it is hard for your child. Who wants to be the teacher's kid? If at all possible, try to avoid this scenario. Sometimes there is no way to not have your own personal child at your school or in your class. Try to be as fair as you can. I know it is hard. There are parents who are too strict and parents who are too lenient. If you have a really good friend at the school, let them try to help you walk that line. And give your child some slack since they absolutely would never choose to be at the same school or in the same class as their parent. So this is hard for everyone. On the plus side, they will probably do all of their homework.

I won't give my son any breaks. As a matter of fact, I'll be harder on him than any other kid. Don't want any favoritism.

Takes too Much Interest with Own Kids with Teachers: Stay out of your children's business. If they need your help they'll ask for it. Don't insert yourself unless you're asked to help either by the teacher or your child. Otherwise, its hands off.

Just give me Johnny's assignment. I'll make sure he does it.

<u>Tells Others How to Teach:</u> Refer to page 93—Stay out of other teacher's business. If they need your help, they'll ask for it. Never undermine another teacher no matter how green they are. ESPECIALLY IN FRONT OF THEIR STUDENTS. NEVER IN FRONT OF THEIR STUDENTS. Don't insert yourself unless you are asked to help either by an administrator or by the teacher.

I'm going to Mrs. Kenley's class during my planning period and help her teach. To show her how it's done.

That's not the way you should teach reading.

True to Yourself in Behavior Management: There are as many behavior management programs out there as there are students in the school. I can't tell you which one is the best, nor would I try. It all has to do with you. If you are not a yeller, then don't try to be in the classroom. The students will see through you. You need to figure out what works best for you as a person. What works best for you is the only behavior management program that you will be able to effectively implement in the classroom. I prefer to do a lot of rewards and concentrate on the positive instead of the negative. Some teachers can control a classroom with a look, others will yell. You might need to do some trial and error to figure out what works best for you. And if what you are doing is not working, then change it. The main thing is that you allow your students to learn. In some lessons where the students are fully engaged your classroom might be a little louder and less organized, but it's okay that it's like that as long as the students are learning. Be positive, you'll figure out what works best for you.

Yelling at students all day will give me a headache and I don't want to have a headache.

U

Uses Students to take care of own Personal Stuff: Be careful and don't use students for your own personal stuff. You are there for a job. Do your job.

Students, I brought my Christmas cards. I need you to address them for me.

Today, we're going to design a flyer for my restaurant.

Billy, I'll give you an 'A' if you cut my lawn this weekend.

V

Vents In the Classroom: Venting in the classroom will ALWAYS backfire. Don't do it. I knew a teacher one time who was let go for the next year not because of her poor teaching, but because of a district mandate. A new policy that all new teachers had to be let go and rehired. After the meeting, the teacher stormed into the classroom and told all of the students she was fired. She ripped down all of her bulletin boards, sat behind her desk, and told the students she wasn't going to teach for the rest of the year. She said that they could do what they wanted as long as they were quiet. You can imagine the complaints the front office heard. Needless to say, all of the teachers were rehired except her. In fact, she was not rehired anywhere in the county because the principal documented what she had done. If you don't know by now, your former boss will be contacted for a recommendation if you've ever taught before. From what I heard, she never taught again and to be completely honest she should have never taught again. Parental complaints dominated the principal's office until the end of the school year. No reason to ever throw a tantrum in class because it might come back and bite you in the butt.

Students, I just got called to the principal's office for my recordkeeping. Can you believe that? How dare she!

1+2=?

W

<u>Way Too Flexible:</u> Don't let students choose whatever they want to do. They will always choose nothing or playing on their phone or games. The only way this works is if you give them specific choices. This is a great way to conduct reviews. The hope is that the student will choose what is easy for them and their learning style. As an added benefit, you actually can learn a lot about your students from their choices or about how they play a game.

You get to choose what you want to do today. Whatever you want.

I want to watch the reality show. I'll watch it on my phone.

<u>Won't Do Anything Unless Gets Credit:</u> Some teachers only do work if they get credit for it. But we as teachers need to be aware that the best way for ALL of us to be successful is for us to work together. I feel like if there is something that I can do for a fellow teacher that will help students, then I should do it whether I get credit for it or not. Shouldn't I be a helper and not a hindrance?

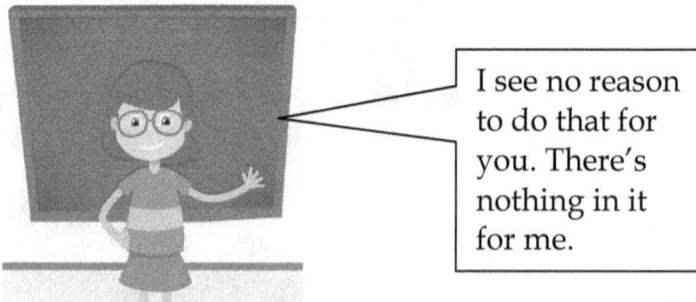

I see no reason to do that for you. There's nothing in it for me.

Whines about Life, School, etc.: There are woes in every person's life. If you look out at that sea of 30 or so students, each one of them could most likely give you a story about how bad their life is on any given day. School is not the place to pour out your woes or complain about money or lack of, or complain about your spouse, or home life. The student's aren't your buddies. They are your charges. You are supposed to teach them. Not burden them.

I don't make enough money to go to the big game. My kids kept me up all night.

Let me tell you what my wife and I argued about last night.

<u>Who Conducts Side Business from School:</u> It's amazing the resources that you have at your disposal as a teacher. If you are in the technology field, you will most likely have access to the latest apps or photo shopping or design building programs. For goodness sakes, don't use your school money to purchase a program that you are dying to use for something personal. It has to have value in the classroom. Buyer beware. There are audits for purchased programs in which you must explain the educational value of said program for the classroom. I knew a teacher whose husband ran a catering business. She was forever incorporating her technology lessons so the students could develop flyers, menus etc. for her personal restaurant. Be careful, even though there are times when this is useful. For example, if you are at a technical school that has an auto repair class, then bringing in a car that needs repairs is the perfect place for the students to practice. Make sure that your school allows this and follow the rules. The last thing you want is for a student to go home and tell their parents that they are working on what is most obviously a personal project of yours with no set rules in place. It is unethical.

Today we are designing the business cards for my side job as a personal trainer.

Who conducts Business Part 2: I can give you an example of one of my favorite students. He was forever coming into the classroom selling candy. You know the candy that is always being sold by band or student council to raise money. The candy is way overpriced and there are various prizes associated with selling a lot. You can get a bicycle if you sell a gazillion bars of candy, but I digress. The point is that I had a rule, no selling in class. I discovered that he kept selling the candy outside of class long after the fund raising was over. It seems this enterprising young man would go home at night, go to the dollar store or a discount store, buy the bars of candy at a discount price, and come back using the same box he used for the band candy and sell his goods. He had made almost a thousand dollars before anyone caught on. He was making a nice living selling rogue candy on the side. So I caution you, school is no place to run a side business. Students will talk and it's unethical. You don't want to be caught using your gifted students. Use caution. Keep those side business as side businesses.

Today, we are making the hors d'oeuvres for the party my business is catering tonight.

# X

XTra Duty: Just as you are not a caretaker for all of your students. You are also not a caretaker for all of your fellow teachers. Quit trying to do for everyone. Just keep up with yourself. Believe me, your responsibilities are enough.

I don't mind. I will do the entire building's duty.

XTra Jobs- Spreads Self Too Thin: I never have understood this one. Some teachers have two or sometimes three jobs. I know that sometimes the money is not that good, but you need to budget and figure out a way to live off the teacher salary at least until you get a good handle on the teaching thing. I know some teachers quit the teaching profession because they can't keep up and sometimes it's not the teaching profession's fault. It's their fault, they take on too much. I've said this more than one time that the first year of teaching is the hardest and if you can get through that you can get through the rest.

I'll plan my lessons as soon as I'm home. I have to leave early for my pet sitting job.

Y

<u>Yes to Everything:</u>   Each teacher has their own class and responsibilities. Don't feel like you have to say yes to every favor thrown your way. Sometimes administrators ask too much. Remember if it is prefaced with a "Can you do me a favor?" then it is not required and you can say no. Say no, if you truly don't have enough time, or if you have an especially hard concept to convey or if you just don't want to take on the extra work. We as teachers have a hard time saying no. Please just do it. SAY NO!!!! It's okay.

Yes, I'll cover for you. Yes, I'll do your duty tomorrow. Yes, you can send your class to me half of the day tomorrow.

Z

Zest For Teaching: I wanted to end on a positive note. I know that I have spent a lot of these telling you what not to do. But remember, we all have a little of some of these undesirable attributes. I hope this gives you something to think about. This — the zest for teaching or as I call it the passion for teaching — should be the first and foremost of your attributes.

I love being a teacher. There is nothing better!

<u>Last Note:</u>

I have spent many years as a teacher and I can tell you as I traveled the world when asked what I do, I proudly acknowledge that I am a teacher and I have never been looked down upon or felt less than. Almost 99% of the time the person looks at me with such admirable respect that it almost makes me cry. Their comments usually range from, "How wonderful! You are so great! I don't know how you do it! I admire you for that!" I have NEVER heard a disparaging remark about me being a teacher. So I tell you with complete certainty that teaching is regarded as one of the noblest professions and if this is the profession you have chosen, then you have chosen well. And you'll never regret it.

# HAPPY TEACHING!!!!

# Appendix

1. Classroom Management: 16, 20, 32, 33, 38,39.40,44,45,46,47,54,55,56,57,59,61,63,64-68,73,74,77,78,79,80,81,84,85-91, 95

2. Lesson Plans: 3, 15,19,20,23, 32,33,38-40, 44-47,54-57,59-61,63-68,70,73,74,76-79, 81, 84-86,89-91

3. Personal Traits: 3, 4, 11, 18, 24, 29, 30,47,51,52,55, 58-61, 63-68,70-74,76-79,81,82,85,86,88-104

4. School Survival: 5, 6, 18, 20, 35, 36, 37,47,51,59,61,64-66,73,75,78,81,85,88-89, 104

5. Negative Traits: 7, 8, 9, 10, 12, 13, 14, 25, 26, 27, 28, 30, 31, 34, 41, 42,47,49,50,53,60,62,69,70,75,83,87-89,94, 96-101

6. Be Careful:  11, 14, 15, 17, 21, 22, 24, 25, 27, 28, 29, 30, 34, 35, 36, 37,41,43-45,47-49,52-55,58-61,69-73,75-77,80-90,92-94,96-103

So if I want to look up about lesson plans I look on those pages?

Yes, and personal traits same thing. Hope I don't see myself too much in the negative traits.

# Other Books by Susan Larned Womble

1) Opal's Brigade ISBN: 978-0-9907600-3-0
2) The Complete Wheel Trilogy ISBN: 978-0-9907600-2-3
3) Newt's World Complete Series ISBM: 978-0-9907600-1-6
4) Bloodstone Legacy ISBN-13: 978-0-9913997-8-5
5) The Big Wheel  ISBN-13: 978-0-9913977-0-9
6) Take The Helm ISBN-13: 978-0-9913977-7-8
7) Battle for the Cure ISBN-13: 978-0-9913977-9-2
8) Newt's World: Beginnings ISBN: 978-0-9913977-1-6
9) Newt's World: Internal Byte ISBN: 978-0-9913977-2-3
10) Newt's World: Beginnings Workbook Teacher's Edition  ISBN: 978-0-9913977-3-0
11) Newt's World: Beginnings Workbook Student's Edition ISBN: 978-0-9913977-4-7
12) Newt's World: Internal Byte Workbook Teacher's Edition ISBN: 978-0-9913977-5-4
13) Newt's World: Internal Byte  Workbook Student's Edition ISBN: 978-0-9913977-6-1

Awards and Notables

• Gold Medal Florida Book Award in children's literature  for "Newt's World: Beginnings"

• Newt's World Beginnings on Just Read Florida Recommended Reading Lists

## ABOUT THE AUTHOR

Susan Larned Womble is an award-winning author. Susan Womble lives in Tallahassee, Florida with her family. She is a retired National Board Certified teacher with a career of teaching in public schools as well as teaching overseas with the Department of Defense European Schools with experience in all grades K-12th in the areas of reading, special education, language arts, math, social studies, and the profoundly handicapped. Visit www.susanwomble.com for more information. Contact her at susan.womble@gmail.com

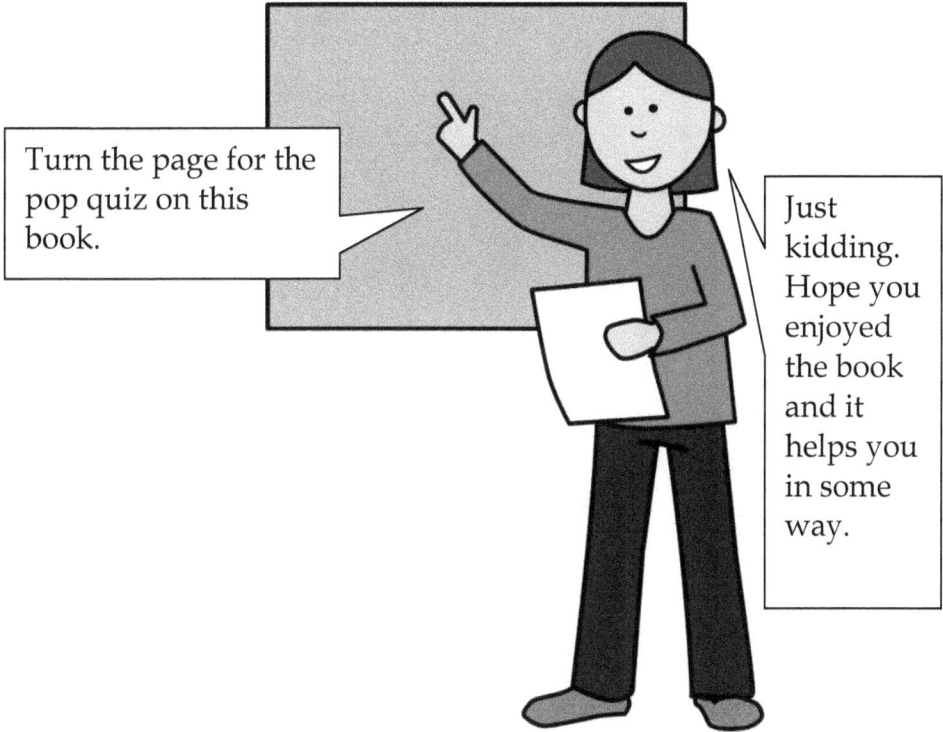

www.ingramcontent.com/pod-product-compliance
Lightning Source LLC
Chambersburg PA
CBHW070519030426
42337CB00016B/2015